greatest ever

# thai

p

This is a Parragon Publishing Book
First published in 2004

Parragon Publishing
Queen Street House
4 Queen Street
Bath BA1 1HE, UK

ISBN: 1-40543-121-0

Printed in Indonesia

Produced by the Bridgewater Book Company Ltd.

**NOTE**

This book uses imperial, metric, and US cup measurements. Follow the same
units of measurement throughout; do not mix imperial and metric.
All spoon measurements are level: teaspoons are assumed to be 5 ml,
and tablespoons are assumed to be 15 ml. Unless otherwise stated,
milk is assumed to be whole, eggs and individual vegetables such as potatoes
are medium, and pepper is freshly ground black pepper.

The times given for each recipe are an approximate guide only,
because the cooking times may vary as a result of the types of oven
and other equipment used.

Recipes using raw or very lightly cooked eggs should be
avoided by infants, the elderly, pregnant women, convalescents, and anyone
suffering from an illness. Pregnant and breast-feeding women are advised to
avoid eating peanuts and peanut products.

# Contents

Introduction                           4

Soups                                  8

Snacks & Appetizers                   28

Fish & Seafood                        64

Meat & Poultry                        88

Rice & Noodles                       134

Vegetables & Salads                  164

Desserts & Drinks                    216

Index                                254

# Introduction

Anyone who loves Thai food will appreciate that it is a unique cuisine, distinctly different from the cooking of the countries which border it, but with many culinary influences from far beyond its geographical frontiers. Thai cooking owes many of its characteristics to climate and culture, but a  history of many centuries of invasions and emigration has played a large part in shaping its cuisine. The roots of the Thai nation can be traced back to the first century A.D., the time of the Chinese Han Dynasty, when the T'ai tribes occupied parts of South China along valuable trade routes between the East and West. Over the years, the T'ai had a close but often stormy relationship with the Chinese, and eventually began to emigrate south to the lands of what is now northern Thailand, bordering Burma and Cambodia, then sparsely occupied by Buddhist and Hindu communities.

In time, the T'ai established the independent Kingdom of Sukhothai (translated as "dawn of happiness"), which eventually became Siam. The ports of Siam were the entrance to an important trade route, and ships from all over Europe and Japan docked there, or sailed inland along the rivers, bringing foreign foods, teas, spices, silks, copper, and ceramics. In the 16th century, the Portuguese introduced the chili to Southeast Asia. The plant flourished immediately in the region's soils and climates, and continues to thrive. Trade with Arab and Indian merchants was important, and many Muslims settled in Siam.

Siam became the Kingdom of Thailand in 1939 after a period of political upheaval, and twenty-first century Thailand still reflects much of her past centuries of mixed cultures, witnessed by the independence, pride, creativity, and passion of the nation. This love of life is apparent in the way they take pleasure

in entertaining and eating. To a visitor, they seem to eat all day long. The streets and waterways are lined with food vendors selling a huge variety of tasty snacks from their stalls, carts, bicycles, and boats.

Parties and celebrations are extremely popular, and during the many festivals, the colorful, often elaborate, and carefully prepared festive foods show a respect for custom and tradition. Visitors are entertained with an unending succession of trays of tasty snacks, platters of exotic fruits, and Thai beer, or local whiskey. When a meal is served, all the dishes are served together, so the cook can enjoy the food along with the guests.

Presenting food beautifully is a source of great pride in Thailand. Vegetables and fruits are sometimes carved into elaborate shapes for use as garnishes—intricate patterns and skilled artistry are an integral part of Thai culture, which exhibits a deep appreciation of all things beautiful.

Everyday life in Thailand is closely tied to the seasons, marked by the harvesting of crops and the vagaries of the monsoon climate. Food is taken seriously, with great care taken in choosing the freshest of ingredients, and thoughtfully balancing delicate flavors and textures. Throughout Thailand, rice is the most important staple food, the center of every meal. And coconut, in its various forms, has an almost equal place. Cooks in every region are expert at making the most of any ingredient available locally, so the character of many classic Thai dishes will vary according to the region in which they are cooked.

# Fundamentals of Thai Cooking

The essential ingredients you need in order to cook Thai food are listed here. Of these, the most important are coconut, lime, chili, rice, garlic, lemongrass, gingerroot, and cilantro. With these you can create many traditional Thai dishes. Although many recipes have long lists of ingredients, the cooking methods involved in making them are simple enough even for inexperienced cooks to follow.

Balance is the guiding principle of Thai cooking, the five extremes of flavor—bitter, sour, hot, salty, and sweet—being carefully and skillfully balanced in each dish and over several courses. Every dish therefore contributes to the balance of the entire meal.

## Basil

Three varieties of sweet basil are used in Thai cooking, but the variety commonly sold in the West also works well. Asian food stores often sell the seeds for Thai basil, so you can grow your own.

## Chilies

The many varieties of chili vary in heat from very mild to fiery hot, so choose carefully. The small red or green Thai chilies are often used—they are very hot, and if you prefer a mild heat, you should remove the seeds. Red chilies are generally slightly sweeter and milder than green chilies. Larger chilies tend to be milder. Dried crushed chilies are used for seasoning.

## Cilantro

This is a herb with a pungent, citrus-like flavor, widely used in savory dishes. It wilts quite quickly, so retains its freshness best if bought with a root attached. Alternatively, you can grow your own. It will make your cooking taste even better.

## Coconut Milk

This is made from grated, pressed fresh coconut. It is sold very widely in cans and longlife packages, in powdered form, and in blocks as creamed

coconut. Coconut cream is skimmed from the top, and is slightly thicker and richer.

## Galangal

A relative of ginger, with a milder, aromatic flavor. It is available fresh or dried.

## Garlic

The pungent cloves of this bulb are used abundantly in Thai cooking. Fresh garlic is used whole, crushed, sliced, or chopped in savory dishes and curry pastes. Pickled garlic can be useful to have in the storecupboard because it makes an attractive garnish.

## Ginger

Fresh gingerroot is peeled and grated, chopped, or sliced for a warm, spicy flavor.

## Kaffir Lime Leaves

These leaves have a distinctive lime scent, and can be bought fresh, dried, or frozen.

## Lemongrass

An aromatic tropical grass with a lemon scent similar to lemon balm. Strip off the fibrous outer leaves and slice or chop the insides finely, or bruise and use whole. It can also be bought in dried, powdered form.

## Palm Sugar

This is a rich, brown, unrefined sugar made from the coconut palm and sold in blocks. The best way to use it is to crush it with a mallet. Turbinado sugar is a good substitute.

## Rice Vinegar

Mirin, or sweet rice vinegar, is a savory flavoring. Sherry or white wine vinegar can be substituted.

## Soy Sauce

Dark and light soy sauce are used for seasoning. The light sauce is saltier than the dark and is used in stir-fries and with light meats. Dark soy adds a rich flavor and color to braised and red meat dishes.

## Tamarind Paste

The pulp of the tamarind fruit is usually sold in blocks. It gives a sour/sweet flavor. Soak the pulp in a bowl of hot water for 30 minutes, then press out the juice and discard the pulp and seeds.

## Thai Curry Paste

This flavoring varies in heat, with yellow the mildest, red variable, and green the hottest.

## Thai Fish Sauce

Called nam pla, this is used like salt for seasoning savory dishes, and has a distinctive, intense aroma.

# Soups

Soups are part of almost every Thai meal, including breakfast. Lunch is often a large bowl of soup—a thin stock-based broth, usually spiked with fresh red or green chilies, and with the addition of fine noodles, rice, egg strips or tiny fish balls, and meat balls or cubes of tofu. In restaurants, soups are often served in a large "firepot" with a central funnel of burning coals to keep the contents hot.

The soups featured in this section are perfect for any time of the day and whatever the occasion, whether it is a formal dinner party or a summer barbecue lunch. They all use traditional Thai ingredients, and the most typical ones can be easily found in Asian food stores and supermarkets.

# chili-spiced shrimp won ton soup

## serves four

**WON TONS**

6 oz/175 g cooked, shelled shrimp

1 garlic clove, crushed

1 scallion, finely chopped

1 tbsp dark soy sauce

1 tbsp Thai fish sauce

1 tbsp chopped cilantro

1 small egg, separated

12 won ton skins

**SOUP**

2 small fresh red Thai chilies

2 scallions

4 cups clear beef stock

1 tbsp Thai fish sauce

1 tbsp dark soy sauce

1 tbsp rice wine or dry sherry

handful of cilantro leaves,
   to garnish

1 Finely chop the shrimp. Place them in a bowl and stir in the garlic, scallion, soy sauce, fish sauce, cilantro, and egg yolk.

2 Lay the won ton skins on a counter in a single layer and place about 1 tablespoon of the filling mixture in the center of each. Brush the edges with egg white and fold each one into a triangle, pressing lightly to seal. Bring the 2 bottom corners of the triangle around to meet in the center, securing with a little egg white to hold in place.

3 To make the soup, slice the chilies at a steep diagonal angle to make long thin slices. Slice the scallions on the same angle.

4 Place the stock, fish sauce, soy sauce, and rice wine in a large pan and bring to a boil. Add the chilies and scallions. Drop the won tons into the pan and simmer for 4–5 minutes, or until thoroughly heated.

5 Serve the soup and won tons in small bowls and garnish with cilantro at the last moment.

# rice soup with eggs

1 tsp corn oil

1 garlic clove, crushed

scant ½ cup ground pork

3 scallions, sliced

1 tbsp grated fresh gingerroot

1 fresh red Thai chili, seeded
  and chopped

4 cups chicken stock

2½ cups cooked long-grain rice

1 tbsp Thai fish sauce

salt and pepper

4 small eggs

2 tbsp shredded cilantro,
  to garnish

1 Heat the oil in a large pan or preheated wok.

2 Add the garlic and pork and stir-fry gently for 1 minute, or until the meat is broken up but not browned.

3 Add the scallions, ginger, chili, and stock, stirring until boiling. Add the rice, then reduce the heat and simmer for 2 minutes.

4 Add the fish sauce and season to taste with salt and pepper. Carefully break the eggs into the soup and simmer over very low heat for 3–4 minutes, or until set.

5 Ladle the soup into large bowls, allowing 1 egg per portion. Garnish with shredded cilantro and serve immediately.

## COOK'S TIP

If you prefer, beat the eggs together and cook like an omelet until set, then cut into ribbon-like strips and add to the soup just before serving.

# tom yam gung

## serves four

1¾ cups light chicken stock

2 fresh kaffir lime leaves, chopped

2-inch/5-cm piece lemongrass, chopped

3 tbsp lemon juice

3 tbsp Thai fish sauce

2 small hot fresh green chilies, seeded and finely chopped

1 tsp sugar

8 small shiitake mushrooms or 8 Chinese straw mushrooms, halved

1 lb/450 g raw shrimp, shelled if necessary and deveined

scallion strips, to garnish

TOM YAM SAUCE

4 tbsp vegetable oil

5 garlic cloves, finely chopped

1 large shallot, finely chopped

2 large hot dried red chilies, roughly chopped

1 tbsp dried shrimp (optional)

1 tbsp Thai fish sauce

2 tsp sugar

1 First make the tom yam sauce. Heat the oil in a pan. Add the garlic and cook for a few seconds until the garlic just browns. Remove with a slotted spoon and reserve. Add the shallot to the same oil and cook until browned and crisp. Remove with a slotted spoon and reserve. Add the chilies and cook until they darken. Remove from the oil and drain on paper towels. Remove the pan from the heat and reserve the oil.

2 Grind the dried shrimp, if using, in a food processor or spice grinder, then add the reserved chilies, garlic, and shallots. Grind to a smooth paste. Return the pan with the original oil to low heat, then add the paste and warm through. Add the fish sauce and sugar and mix. Remove the pan from the heat.

3 Heat the stock and 2 tablespoons of the tom yam sauce together in a separate pan. Add the lime leaves, lemongrass, lemon juice, fish sauce, chilies, and sugar and simmer for 2 minutes.

4 Add the mushrooms and shrimp and cook for an additional 2–3 minutes, or until the shrimp are cooked. Ladle into warmed serving bowls and serve immediately, garnished with scallion strips.

# thai-style seafood soup

5 cups fish stock

1 lemongrass stem,
    split lengthwise

pared rind of ½ lime or 1 fresh
    kaffir lime leaf

1-inch/2.5-cm piece fresh
    gingerroot, sliced

¼ tsp chili paste, or to taste

4–6 scallions

7 oz/200 g large or medium raw
    shrimp, shelled

salt

9 oz/250 g scallops (16–20)

2 tbsp cilantro leaves

finely chopped red bell pepper or
    fresh red chili rings, to garnish

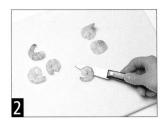

1 Place the stock in a pan with the lemongrass, lime rind, ginger, and chili paste. Bring just to a boil, then reduce the heat and simmer, covered, for 10–15 minutes.

2 Cut the scallions in half lengthwise, then slice crosswise very thinly. Cut the shrimp almost in half lengthwise, keeping the tails intact. Devein if necessary.

3 Pour the stock through a strainer, then return to the pan and bring to a simmer, with bubbles rising at the edges and the surface trembling. Add the scallions and cook for 2–3 minutes. Taste and season with salt, if needed. Stir in a little more chili paste if wished.

4 Add the scallops and shrimp and poach for 1 minute, or until they turn opaque and the shrimp curl.

5 Drop in the cilantro leaves, then ladle the soup into warmed serving bowls, dividing the shellfish evenly, and garnish with bell pepper or chili rings.

## VARIATION

If you have light chicken stock, but no fish stock, it will make an equally tasty though different version of this soup.

# hot & sour soup

## serves four

12 oz/350 g raw or cooked shrimp
    in shells
1 tbsp vegetable oil
1 lemongrass stem,
    coarsely chopped
2 fresh kaffir lime leaves, shredded
1 fresh green chili, seeded
    and chopped
5 cups chicken or fish stock
1 lime
1 tbsp Thai fish sauce
salt and pepper
1 fresh red Thai chili, seeded and
    thinly sliced
1 scallion, thinly sliced
1 tbsp finely chopped cilantro,
    to garnish

### COOK'S TIP

To devein the shrimp, remove the
shells. Cut a slit along the back
of each shrimp and remove the
fine black vein that runs along
the length of the back. Wipe with
paper towels.

1 Peel the shrimp and reserve the shells. Devein the shrimp (see Cook's Tip), then cover with plastic wrap and let chill in the refrigerator.

2 Heat the oil in a large, heavy-bottom pan. Add the shrimp shells and stir-fry for 3–4 minutes, or until they turn pink. Add the lemongrass, lime leaves, chili, and stock. Pare a thin strip of rind from the lime and grate the rest. Add the grated rind to the pan.

3 Bring to a boil, then reduce the heat and let simmer, covered, for 20 minutes.

4 Strain the liquid and pour it back into the pan. Squeeze the juice from the lime and add to the pan with the fish sauce and salt and pepper to taste.

5 Bring to a boil, then reduce the heat and add the shrimp. Simmer for 2–3 minutes.

6 Add the thinly sliced chili and scallion. Sprinkle with the chopped cilantro and serve.

15

# chicken noodle soup

## serves four–six

1 sheet dried egg noodles from a
  9 oz/250 g package

1 tbsp corn oil

4 skinless, boneless chicken
  thighs, diced

1 bunch of scallions, sliced

2 garlic cloves, chopped

¾-inch/2-cm piece fresh gingerroot,
  finely chopped

3¾ cups chicken stock

generous ¾ cup coconut milk

3 tsp Thai red curry paste

3 tbsp peanut butter

2 tbsp light soy sauce

salt and pepper

1 small red bell pepper, seeded
  and chopped

½ cup frozen peas

### VARIATION

You can use other types
of noodles in this soup, such
as rice or cellophane noodles.
Prepare according to the
package directions.

1 Place the noodles in a shallow
heatproof dish and let soak in
boiling water according to the
package directions.

2 Heat the oil in a large, heavy-
bottom pan or preheated wok.
Add the chicken and stir-fry for
5 minutes, or until lightly browned.
Add the white part of the scallions,
the garlic, and ginger and stir-fry for
2 minutes.

3 Add the stock, coconut milk, curry
paste, peanut butter, and soy
sauce. Season to taste with salt and
pepper. Bring to a boil, stirring
constantly, then simmer for 8 minutes,
stirring occasionally. Add the bell
pepper, peas, and green scallion tops
and cook for an additional 2 minutes.

4 Add the drained noodles and
heat through. Spoon into warmed
serving bowls and serve immediately.

# chicken & coconut milk soup

## serves four

1¾ cups canned coconut milk

generous 2 cups chicken stock

6 thin slices fresh galangal

2 lemongrass stems, bruised

4 fresh kaffir lime leaves

8 oz/225 g chicken breast fillets

4 scallions

2 fresh red chilies, seeded and
   finely sliced

4 tbsp Thai fish sauce

2 tbsp lime juice

2 tbsp chopped cilantro

1 Place the coconut milk, stock, galangal, lemongrass, and lime leaves in a large pan and bring to a boil.

2 Cut the chicken into strips and add to the pan. Reduce the heat and simmer for 10 minutes, or until the chicken is cooked.

3 Slice the scallions and add to the pan with the chilies. Simmer for an additional 3 minutes. Stir in the fish sauce, lime juice, and cilantro and serve in warmed bowls.

# spicy thai soup with shrimp

## serves four

2 tbsp tamarind paste

4 fresh red Thai chilies,
 very finely chopped

2 garlic cloves, crushed

1-inch/2.5-cm piece fresh galangal,
 very finely chopped

4 tbsp Thai fish sauce

2 tbsp palm sugar or
 superfine sugar

8 fresh kaffir lime leaves,
 coarsely torn

4 cups fish stock

1 cup very thinly sliced carrots

2 cups diced sweet potato

3½ oz/100 g baby corn cobs,
 halved

3 tbsp cilantro, coarsely chopped

3½ oz/100 g cherry tomatoes,
 halved

8 oz/225 g cooked fantail shrimp

1 Place the tamarind paste, chilies, garlic, galangal, fish sauce, sugar, lime leaves, and stock in a large, preheated wok. Bring to a boil, stirring constantly.

2 Reduce the heat and add the carrots, sweet potato, and baby corn cobs to the mixture in the wok.

### COOK'S TIP

Galangal or Thai ginger is a member of the ginger family, but it is yellow in color with pink sprouts. The flavor is aromatic and less pungent than ginger.

3 Let the soup simmer, uncovered, for 10 minutes, or until the vegetables are just tender.

4 Stir the cilantro, cherry tomatoes, and shrimp into the soup and heat through for 5 minutes.

5 Transfer the soup to warmed serving bowls and serve hot.

# mushroom & tofu broth

### serves four

4 dried shiitake mushrooms

⅔ cup boiling water

1 tbsp corn oil

1 tsp sesame oil

1 garlic clove, crushed

1 fresh green chili, seeded and
finely chopped

6 scallions, sliced

1½ cups sliced oyster mushrooms

2 fresh kaffir lime leaves,
finely shredded

4 cups rich brown stock

2 tbsp lime juice

1 tbsp rice vinegar or white
wine vinegar

1 tbsp Thai fish sauce

3 oz/85 g firm tofu (drained weight),
diced

salt and pepper

1 Place the dried shiitake mushrooms in a heatproof bowl and pour over the boiling water. Let soak for 30 minutes. Drain, reserving the liquid, then coarsely chop the black mushrooms.

2 Heat the oils in a large pan or preheated wok over high heat. Add the garlic, chili, and scallions and stir-fry for 1 minute, or until softened but not browned.

3 Add all of the mushrooms, lime leaves, stock, and reserved mushroom liquid. Bring to a boil.

**COOK'S TIP**

Use a clear, richly colored homemade beef stock, or a Japanese dashi, to make an attractive clear broth. Bouillon cubes generally make a cloudy stock. To make a vegetarian version of the broth, use a well-flavored vegetable stock and replace the fish sauce with light soy sauce.

4 Stir in the lime juice, rice vinegar, and fish sauce, then reduce the heat and let simmer gently for 3–4 minutes.

5 Add the diced tofu and season to taste with salt and pepper. Heat gently until boiling, then ladle into warmed serving bowls and serve.

# aromatic chicken & vegetable soup

## serves four

½ lime

handful of cilantro

4 cups chicken stock

1 lemongrass stem, bruised

1 small fresh red chili

salt and pepper

8 oz/225 g chicken breast fillet

1 carrot

1 cup snow peas, cut into thin
    diagonal strips

3½ oz/100 g baby corn cobs,
    thinly sliced

4 scallions, thinly sliced

1 Grate the lime. Strip the cilantro leaves from the stems. Reserve the leaves and place the stems in a pan with the stock, lemongrass, chili, and lime rind. Bring to a boil, then cover and simmer for 15 minutes.

2 Strain the stock into a separate pan. Squeeze in the lime juice and add salt and pepper to taste.

3 Dice the chicken and add to the stock. Bring to a boil, then simmer for 5 minutes. Cut the carrot into ribbons and add to the pan with the snow peas and corn. Simmer for 2 minutes, or until the vegetables are tender and the chicken is cooked.

4 Coarsely chop the cilantro leaves and stir into the soup with the scallions. Serve immediately.

21

# chilled avocado, lime & cilantro soup

## serves four

2 ripe avocados

1 small mild onion, chopped

1 garlic clove, crushed

2 tbsp chopped cilantro

1 tbsp chopped fresh mint

2 tbsp lime juice

3 cups vegetable stock

1 tbsp rice vinegar or white
  wine vinegar

1 tbsp light soy sauce

salt and pepper

TO GARNISH

2 tbsp sour cream

1 tbsp finely chopped cilantro

2 tsp lime juice

finely shredded lime rind

1 Halve and pit the avocados, then scoop out the flesh. Place in a food processor or blender with the onion, garlic, cilantro, mint, lime juice, and about half the stock and process until completely smooth.

2 Add the remaining stock, rice vinegar, and soy sauce and process again to mix well. Taste and adjust the seasoning if necessary, or add a little extra lime juice if required. Cover and let chill in the refrigerator.

3 To make the lime and cilantro cream garnish, mix the sour cream, cilantro, and lime juice together in a small bowl. Spoon into the soup just before serving and sprinkle with shredded lime rind.

# creamy corn soup with egg

## serves four

1 tbsp vegetable oil

3 garlic cloves, crushed

1 tsp grated fresh gingerroot

3 cups chicken stock

13 oz/375 g canned creamed corn

1 tbsp Thai fish sauce

6 oz/175 g canned white
    crabmeat, drained

salt and pepper

1 egg

TO GARNISH

shredded cilantro

paprika

1 Heat the oil in a large, heavy-bottom pan. Add the garlic and cook for 1 minute, stirring constantly.

2 Add the ginger to the pan, then stir in the stock and creamed corn. Bring to a boil.

3 Stir in the fish sauce, crabmeat, and salt and pepper to taste. Return the soup to a boil.

4 Beat the egg in a small bowl, then stir lightly into the soup so that it sets into long strands. Simmer gently for 30 seconds, or until just set.

5 Ladle the soup into serving bowls and serve hot, garnished with shredded cilantro and paprika sprinkled over the surface.

### VARIATION

To give the soup an extra rich flavor kick for a special occasion, stir in 1 tablespoon of rice wine or dry sherry just before you ladle it into bowls.

# pumpkin & coconut soup

### serves six

2 lb 4 oz/1 kg pumpkin

1 tbsp peanut oil

1 tsp yellow mustard seeds

1 garlic clove, crushed

1 large onion, chopped

1 celery stalk, chopped

1 small fresh red chili, chopped

3¾ cups chicken stock

1 tbsp dried shrimp

5 tbsp coconut cream

salt and pepper

1 Using a sharp knife, halve the pumpkin and remove the seeds. Cut away the skin and dice the flesh.

2 Heat the oil in a large, flameproof casserole. Add the mustard seeds and cook until they begin to pop. Stir in the garlic, onion, celery, and chili and stir-fry for 1–2 minutes.

3 Add the pumpkin with the stock and dried shrimp to the casserole and bring to a boil. Reduce the heat, then cover and simmer for 30 minutes, or until the ingredients are very tender.

4 Transfer the mixture to a food processor or blender and process until smooth. Return to the casserole and stir in the coconut cream.

5 Season to taste with salt and pepper and serve hot.

### COOK'S TIP

For an extra touch, swirl a spoonful of thick coconut milk into each bowl before serving.

# spinach & ginger soup

## serves four

2 tbsp corn oil

1 onion, chopped

2 garlic cloves, finely chopped

1-inch/2.5-cm piece fresh
   gingerroot, finely chopped

3 cups fresh young
   spinach leaves

1 small lemongrass stem,
   finely chopped

4 cups chicken or
   vegetable stock

1 small potato, chopped

1 tbsp rice wine or dry sherry

salt and pepper

1 tsp sesame oil

---

### VARIATION

To make a creamy-textured
spinach and coconut soup, stir in
4 tablespoons of creamed
coconut, or alternatively replace
1¼ cups of the stock with
coconut milk. Serve the soup
with shavings of fresh coconut
sprinkled over the surface.

1 Heat the corn oil in a large pan. Add the onion, garlic, and ginger and stir-fry gently for 3–4 minutes, or until softened but not browned.

2 Reserve 2–3 small spinach leaves. Add the remaining leaves and lemongrass to the pan, stirring until the spinach is wilted. Add the stock and potato to the pan and bring to a boil. Reduce the heat, then cover and simmer for 10 minutes.

3 Transfer the soup to a food processor or blender and process until completely smooth.

4 Return the soup to the pan and add the rice wine, then adjust the seasoning to taste with salt and pepper. Heat until just about to boil.

5 Finely shred the reserved spinach leaves and sprinkle some over the top. Drizzle with a few drops of sesame oil and serve hot, garnished with the remaining finely shredded spinach leaves.

# Snacks & Appetizers

The structure of a Thai meal is more flexible than in the West, with no first courses and entrées as such; instead, snacks or appetizers may be served in the afternoon or offered to guests before they sit down to eat a formal meal.

Many of the recipes in this section are savory snacks that are eaten at all times of the day as well as at parties and celebrations. The Thais eat when they are hungry, and street vendors cater for this need with a huge and tempting array of wares from their stalls and bicycles—each street vendor has his own specialty of fast food, from crab cakes to spare ribs, and from steamed mussels to rice soup.

# jumbo shrimp rolls with sweet soy sauce

## serves four

DIP

1 small fresh red Thai chili, seeded

1 tsp clear honey

4 tbsp soy sauce

SHRIMP ROLLS

2 tbsp cilantro leaves

1 garlic clove

1½ tsp Thai red curry paste

16 won ton skins

1 egg white, lightly beaten

16 raw jumbo shrimp, shelled and

　　tails left intact

corn oil, for deep-frying

1 To make the dip, finely chop the chili and place in a small bowl. Add the honey and soy sauce and stir well. Reserve until required.

2 To make the shrimp rolls, finely chop the cilantro and garlic and place in a bowl. Add the curry paste and mix well.

3 Brush each won ton skin with egg white and place a small dab of the cilantro mixture in the center. Place a shrimp on top.

4 Fold the won ton skin over, enclosing the shrimp and leaving the tail exposed. Repeat with the other shrimp.

5 Heat the oil for deep-frying in a large, heavy-bottom pan to 350°–375°F/180°–190°C, or until a cube of bread browns in 30 seconds. Deep-fry the shrimp in small batches for 1–2 minutes each, or until golden brown and crisp. Drain on paper towels and serve with the dip.

# fish cakes with hot peanut dip

### serves four–five

12 oz/350 g skinless white fish fillet,
   such as cod or haddock

1 tbsp Thai fish sauce

2 tsp Thai red curry paste

1 tbsp lime juice

1 garlic clove, crushed

4 dried kaffir lime leaves, crumbled

1 egg white

3 tbsp chopped cilantro

vegetable oil, for pan-frying

salad greens, to serve

PEANUT DIP

1 small fresh red chili

1 tbsp light soy sauce

1 tbsp lime juice

1 tbsp brown sugar

3 tbsp chunky peanut butter

4 tbsp coconut milk

salt and pepper

snipped fresh chives, to garnish

1 Place the fish fillet in a food processor with the fish sauce, curry paste, lime juice, garlic, lime leaves, and egg white and process to a smooth paste.

2 Stir in the cilantro and quickly process again until mixed. Divide the mixture into 8–10 pieces and roll into balls, then flatten to make round patties. Reserve.

3 To make the dip, halve and seed the chili, then chop finely. Place in a small pan with the remaining dip ingredients and heat gently, stirring constantly, until well blended. Adjust the seasoning to taste, if necessary, and transfer to a small bowl. Garnish with snipped chives and reserve until required.

4 Heat the oil for pan-frying in a wide skillet until very hot. Pan-fry the fish cakes in batches for 3–4 minutes on each side, or until golden brown. Drain on paper towels and serve them hot on a bed of salad greens with the peanut dip.

# shrimp & chicken sesame toasts

## makes seventy-two pieces

4 skinless, boneless
   chicken thighs

3½ oz/100 g cooked,
   shelled shrimp

1 small egg, beaten

3 scallions, finely chopped

2 garlic cloves, crushed

2 tbsp chopped cilantro

1 tbsp Thai fish sauce

½ tsp pepper

¼ tsp salt

12 slices white bread,
   crusts removed

½ cup sesame seeds

corn oil, for pan-frying

shredded scallion curls,
   to garnish (see page 212)

1 Place the chicken and shrimp in a food processor and process until very finely chopped. Add the egg, scallions, garlic, cilantro, fish sauce, pepper, and salt and pulse for a few seconds to mix well. Transfer the mixture to a large bowl.

2 Spread the mixture evenly over the slices of bread, right to the edges. Sprinkle the sesame seeds over a plate and press the spread side of each slice of bread into them to coat evenly.

3 Using a sharp knife, cut the bread into small rectangles, making 6 per slice.

4 Heat a 1-cm/½-inch depth of oil in a wide skillet until very hot. Pan-fry the bread rectangles quickly in batches for 2–3 minutes, or until golden brown, turning them over once.

5 Drain the toasts well on paper towels, then transfer to a serving dish and garnish with shredded scallion curls. Serve hot.

# jumbo shrimp skewers

## serves two as an entrée or four as an appetizer

12 raw jumbo shrimp in shells

3 oranges

MARINADE

1-inch/2.5-cm piece fresh gingerroot

3 garlic cloves, crushed

2 shallots, finely chopped

1 lemongrass stem, finely chopped

1 fresh red chili, finely chopped

pinch of salt

1 tbsp lime juice

1 tbsp soy sauce

2 tbsp rice wine or dry sherry

TO GARNISH

cilantro sprigs

lime wedges

1 To make the marinade, grate the ginger and place in a food processor with the garlic, shallots, lemongrass, chili, salt, lime juice, soy sauce, and rice wine. Process until smooth, then transfer the mixture to a shallow bowl.

2 Using a small knife or scissors, split the shrimp shells down the back, but leave attached. Devein if necessary. Add to the marinade. Cover with plastic wrap and let marinate in the refrigerator for at least 30 minutes and up to 1 hour.

3 Preheat the broiler to medium. Thread each shrimp on to a presoaked bamboo skewer (see Cook's Tip, page 82), inserting the skewer at the tail and coming out at the head end until the pointed end extends at least 3 inches/7.5 cm beyond the shrimp.

4 Broil for 2 minutes on each side, or until the shrimp are pink and cooked through. Insert the skewers in the oranges, then transfer to a plate and garnish with the cilantro sprigs and lime wedges. Serve.

# open crabmeat sandwich

## serves two

2 tbsp lime juice

¾-inch/2-cm piece fresh gingerroot, grated

¾-inch/2-cm piece lemongrass, finely chopped

5 tbsp mayonnaise

2 large slices crusty bread

1 ripe avocado

5½ oz/150 g cooked crabmeat

pepper

cilantro sprigs, to garnish

lime wedges, to serve

1 Mix 1 tablespoon of the lime juice, the ginger, and lemongrass together in a small bowl. Add the mayonnaise and mix well.

2 Spread 1 tablespoon of the mayonnaise smoothly over each slice of bread.

3 Halve the avocado and remove the pit. Peel and slice the flesh thinly, then arrange the slices on the bread. Sprinkle with a little of the remaining lime juice.

4 Spoon the crabmeat over the avocado, then add the remaining lime juice. Spoon over the remaining mayonnaise, then season with pepper to taste and top with a cilantro sprig. Serve immediately with lime wedges.

### COOK'S TIP

To make homemade lime- and ginger-flavored mayonnaise, place 2 egg yolks, 1 tablespoon lime juice, and ½ teaspoon grated fresh gingerroot in a food processor or blender and blend briefly. With the motor running, gradually add 1¼ cups olive oil, drop by drop, until the mixture is thick and smooth. Season to taste with salt and pepper.

# crab omelet

## serves four

8 oz/225 g cooked fresh white
    crabmeat, or thawed if frozen

3 scallions, finely chopped

1 tbsp chopped cilantro

1 tbsp snipped fresh chives

pinch of cayenne pepper

2 tbsp vegetable oil

2 garlic cloves, crushed

1 tsp grated fresh gingerroot

1 fresh red chili, seeded and
    finely chopped

2 tbsp lime juice

2 fresh kaffir lime leaves, shredded

2 tsp sugar

2 tsp Thai fish sauce

3 eggs

4 tbsp coconut cream

1 tsp salt

scallion strips, to garnish

### COOK'S TIP

You can also serve this omelet
warm. After adding the crab
mixture, cook for 3–4 minutes to
let the mixture heat through,
then serve immediately.

1 Place the crabmeat in a bowl and check for any small pieces of shell. Add the scallions, cilantro, chives, and cayenne and reserve.

2 Heat half the oil in a skillet or preheated wok. Add the garlic, ginger, and chili and stir-fry for 30 seconds. Add the lime juice, lime leaves, sugar, and fish sauce. Simmer for 3–4 minutes, or until reduced. Remove from the heat and let cool. Add to the crab mixture and reserve.

3 Lightly beat the eggs with the coconut cream and salt. Heat the remaining oil in a skillet over medium heat. Add the egg mixture and, as it sets on the bottom, carefully pull the edges in toward the center, letting the unset egg run underneath.

4 When the egg is nearly set, spoon the crab mixture down the center and fold the sides over. Cook for an additional 1–2 minutes to finish cooking the egg, then turn the omelet out of the skillet on to a serving dish. Let cool, then chill for 2–3 hours or overnight. Cut into 4 pieces, then garnish with scallion strips and serve.

# steamed crab cakes

## serves four

1–2 banana leaves

2 garlic cloves, crushed

1 tsp finely chopped lemongrass

½ tsp pepper

2 tbsp chopped cilantro

3 tbsp creamed coconut

1 tbsp lime juice

7 oz/200 g cooked crabmeat, flaked

1 tbsp Thai fish sauce

2 egg whites

1 egg yolk

8 cilantro leaves

corn oil, for deep-frying

chili dipping sauce, to serve

1 Use the banana leaves to line 8 x ½-cup ramekin dishes or foil containers.

2 Mix the garlic, lemongrass, pepper, and cilantro together in a bowl. Place the creamed coconut and lime juice in a separate bowl and mash until smooth. Stir the 2 mixtures together and add the crabmeat and fish sauce.

3 Whisk the egg whites in a clean, greasefree bowl until stiff, then lightly and evenly fold them into the crab mixture.

4 Spoon the mixture into the prepared ramekin dishes or foil containers and press down lightly. Brush the tops with egg yolk and top each with a cilantro leaf.

5 Place in a steamer half filled with boiling water, then cover with a lid and steam for 15 minutes, or until firm to the touch. Pour off the excess liquid and remove from the ramekin dishes or foil containers.

6 Heat the oil for deep-frying in a large, heavy-bottom pan to 350–375°F/180–190°C, or until a cube of bread browns in 30 seconds. Add the crab cakes and deep-fry for 1 minute, turning them over once, until golden brown. Serve hot with a chili dipping sauce.

# potato crab cakes

## serves four

1 lb/450 g mealy potatoes, diced

6 oz/175 g cooked white crabmeat,
    drained if canned

4 scallions, chopped

1 tsp light soy sauce

½ tsp sesame oil

1 tsp chopped lemongrass

1 tsp lime juice

3 tbsp all-purpose flour, plus extra
    for dusting

salt and pepper

2 tbsp vegetable oil

SAUCE

4 tbsp finely chopped cucumber

2 tbsp clear honey

1 tbsp garlic wine vinegar

½ tsp light soy sauce

1 fresh red chili, chopped

TO GARNISH

1 fresh red chili, sliced

cucumber slices

### COOK'S TIP

Do not make the cucumber sauce
too far in advance because
the water from the cucumber
will make the sauce runny and
dilute the flavor.

1 Cook the diced potatoes in a
large pan of boiling water for
10 minutes, or until cooked through.
Drain well and mash.

2 Mix the crabmeat into the potato
with the scallions, soy sauce,
sesame oil, lemongrass, lime juice,
and flour. Season to taste with salt
and pepper.

3 Divide the potato mixture into
8 equal-size portions and shape
them into small patties, using
floured hands.

4 Heat the vegetable oil in a
preheated wok or skillet. Add the
crab cakes, 4 at a time, and cook for
5–7 minutes, turning once. Keep warm
and repeat with the remaining cakes.

5 Meanwhile, make the sauce. Mix
the cucumber, honey, vinegar, soy
sauce, and chopped chili together in a
small serving bowl.

6 Garnish the crab cakes with the
sliced chili and cucumber slices
and serve with the sauce.

# mussels in spiced batter

## serves four

40 large live mussels in shells

2 tbsp all-purpose flour

2 tbsp rice flour

½ tsp salt

1 tbsp dry unsweetened coconut

1 egg white

1 tbsp rice wine or dry sherry

2 tbsp water

1 small fresh red Thai chili, seeded
   and chopped

1 tbsp chopped cilantro

corn oil, for deep-frying

lime wedges, to serve

1 Clean the mussels by scrubbing or scraping the shells and pulling out any beards that are attached to them. Discard any with broken shells or any that refuse to close when tapped.

2 Place the mussels in a large pan with just the water that clings to their shells and cook, covered, over high heat for 3–4 minutes, shaking the pan occasionally, until they have opened. Drain well, let cool slightly, then remove from the shells. Discard any mussels that remain closed.

3 To make the batter, sift the all-purpose flour, rice flour, and salt into a large bowl. Add the coconut, egg white, rice wine, and water and beat until well mixed and a batter forms. Stir the chili and cilantro into the batter.

4 Heat a 2-inch/5-cm depth of oil for deep-frying in a large, heavy-bottom pan to 350–375°F/180–190°C, or until a cube of bread browns in 30 seconds. Holding the mussels with a fork, dip them quickly into the batter, then drop into the hot oil and deep-fry for 1–2 minutes, or until crisp and golden brown.

5 Drain the mussels on paper towels and serve hot with lime wedges to squeeze over.

### COOK'S TIP

If you reserve the mussel shells, the cooked mussels can be replaced in them to serve.

# fragrant mussels

## serves two as an entrée or four as an appetizer

2 lb 4 oz/1 kg live mussels in shells

3 fresh or dried kaffir lime leaves

2 tbsp water

1 lemongrass stem, bruised

2 garlic cloves, crushed

generous ¾ cup coconut cream

2 tbsp chopped cilantro

salt and pepper

warmed crusty bread,
    to serve

1 Clean the mussels by scrubbing or scraping the shells and pulling out any beards that are attached. Discard any with broken shells or any that refuse to close when tapped.

2 Chop the lime leaves and place in a large pan with the water, lemongrass, and garlic. Heat until boiling. Add the mussels, then cover and cook for 3–4 minutes, or until they have opened. Discard any mussels that remain closed. Transfer to a serving dish, cover, and place in a low oven.

3 Boil the cooking liquid hard until reduced by half, then stir in the coconut cream. Boil to reduce and thicken slightly. Stir in the cilantro and add salt and pepper to taste.

4 Pour over the mussels and serve with warmed crusty bread.

# steamed mussels with lemongrass & basil

### serves two as an entrée or four as an appetizer

2 lb 4 oz/1 kg live mussels in shells

2 shallots, finely chopped

1 lemongrass stem, finely sliced

1 garlic clove, finely chopped

3 tbsp rice wine or dry sherry

2 tbsp lime juice

1 tbsp Thai fish sauce

4 tbsp chopped fresh basil

salt and pepper

2 tbsp butter

fresh basil leaves, to garnish

crusty bread, to serve

---

**COOK'S TIP**

Fresh clams in shells are also
very good when cooked
by this method.

---

1 Clean the mussels by scrubbing or scraping the shells and pulling out any beards that are attached to them. Discard any with broken shells or any that refuse to close when tapped.

2 Place the shallots, lemongrass, garlic, rice wine, lime juice, and fish sauce in a large, heavy-bottom pan and place over high heat.

3 Add the mussels, then cover and steam for 3–4 minutes, shaking the pan occasionally, until the mussels have opened.

4 Discard any mussels that remain closed, then stir in the chopped basil and season to taste with salt and pepper.

5 Scoop out the mussels with a slotted spoon and divide between 4 deep bowls. Quickly whisk the butter into the pan juices, then pour the juices over the mussels.

6 Garnish each bowl with fresh basil leaves and serve with plenty of crusty bread to mop up the juices.

# roasted spare ribs with honey & soy

## serves four

2 lb 4 oz/1 kg Chinese-style
spare ribs

½ lemon

½ small orange

1-inch/2.5-cm piece fresh
gingerroot

2 garlic cloves

1 small onion, chopped

2 tbsp soy sauce

2 tbsp rice wine or dry sherry

½ tsp Thai seven-spice powder

2 tbsp clear honey

1 tbsp sesame oil

lemon twists, to garnish

orange wedges, to serve

1 Preheat the oven to 350°F/180°C. Place the spare ribs in a wide roasting pan, then cover loosely with foil and cook for 30 minutes.

2 Meanwhile, remove any seeds from the lemon and orange and place them in a food processor with the ginger, garlic, onion, soy sauce, rice wine, seven-spice powder, honey, and oil. Process until smooth.

3 Increase the oven temperature to 400°F/200°C. Pour off any fat from the spare ribs, then spoon the puréed mixture over the spare ribs and toss to coat evenly.

4 Return the ribs to the oven and roast for 40 minutes, turning and basting them occasionally, until golden brown. Garnish with lemon twists and serve hot with orange wedges.

# crispy pork & peanut baskets

## serves four

2 sheets phyllo pastry, about 16½ x
    11 inches/42 x 28 cm each
1 tbsp vegetable oil, plus extra
    for brushing
1 garlic clove, crushed
generous 1 cup ground pork
1 tsp Thai red curry paste
2 scallions, finely chopped
3 tbsp chunky peanut butter
1 tbsp light soy sauce
1 tbsp chopped cilantro
salt and pepper
cilantro sprigs, to garnish

1 Preheat the oven to 400°F/200°C. Cut each sheet of phyllo pastry into 24 x 2¾-inch/7-cm squares, to make a total of 48 squares. Brush each square lightly with oil and arrange the squares in stacks of 4 in 12 small patty pans, pointing outward. Press the pastry down into the pans.

2 Bake the pastry shells in the preheated oven for 6–8 minutes, or until golden brown.

3 Meanwhile, heat 1 tablespoon of oil in a heavy-bottom skillet. Add the garlic and cook for 30 seconds, then stir in the pork and stir-fry over high heat for 4–5 minutes, or until the meat is golden brown.

4 Add the curry paste and scallions and continue to stir-fry for an additional 1 minute, then stir in the peanut butter, soy sauce, and cilantro. Season to taste with salt and pepper.

5 Spoon the pork mixture into the phyllo baskets, then garnish with cilantro sprigs and serve hot.

## COOK'S TIP

When using phyllo pastry, remember that it dries out very quickly and becomes brittle and difficult to handle. Work quickly and cover any sheets of pastry you're not using with plastic wrap and a dampened cloth.

# lemongrass chicken skewers

## serves four

2 long or 4 short lemongrass stems

2 large skinless, boneless chicken
   breasts, about 14 oz/400 g
   in total

1 small egg white

1 carrot, finely grated

1 small fresh red chili, seeded
   and chopped

2 tbsp snipped fresh garlic chives

2 tbsp chopped cilantro

salt and pepper

1 tbsp corn oil

TO GARNISH

cilantro sprigs

lime slices

mixed salad greens, to serve

1 If the lemongrass stems are long, cut them in half across the center to make 4 short lengths. Cut each stem in half lengthwise, so that you have 8 sticks.

2 Coarsely chop the chicken pieces and place them in a food processor with the egg white. Process to a smooth paste, then add the carrot, chili, chives, cilantro, and salt and pepper to taste. Process for a few seconds to mix well. Transfer the mixture to a large bowl. Cover and chill in the refrigerator for 15 minutes.

3 Preheat the broiler to medium. Divide the mixture into 8 equal-size portions and use your hands to shape the mixture around the lemongrass "skewers."

### VARIATION

If you can't find whole lemongrass stems, use presoaked wooden skewers instead (see Cook's Tip, page 82), and add ½ teaspoon ground lemongrass to the mixture with the other flavorings.

4 Brush the skewers with oil and cook under the hot broiler for 4–6 minutes, turning them occasionally, until golden brown and thoroughly cooked. Alternatively, grill over medium–hot coals.

5 Transfer to serving plates. Garnish with cilantro sprigs and lime slices and serve hot with salad greens.

# steamed won ton bundles

## serves four

generous 1 cup ground pork

1 tbsp dried shrimp, finely chopped

1 fresh green chili, finely chopped

2 shallots, finely chopped

1 tsp cornstarch

1 small egg, beaten

2 tsp dark soy sauce

2 tsp rice wine or dry sherry

salt and pepper

12 won ton skins

1 tsp sesame oil

chili dipping sauce, to serve

1 Mix the pork, dried shrimp, chili, and shallots together in a bowl. Blend the cornstarch with half the egg and stir into the pork mixture with the soy sauce and rice wine. Season to taste with salt and pepper.

2 Arrange the won ton skins flat on a clean counter and place 1 tablespoon of the pork mixture on to the center of each skin.

3 Brush the skins with the remaining egg and carefully pull up the edges, pinching together lightly at the top and leaving a small gap so that the filling can just be seen.

4 Place enough water in the bottom of a steamer and bring to a boil. Brush the inside of the top part of the steamer with the oil.

5 Arrange the won tons in the top, then cover and steam for 15–20 minutes. Serve hot with a chili dipping sauce.

# stuffed chicken wings

## serves four

8 chicken wings

3 tbsp dried shrimp

3 tbsp hot water

1¾ cups ground pork

1 garlic clove, crushed

1 tbsp Thai fish sauce

½ tsp salt

½ tsp pepper

2 scallions, finely chopped

¼ tsp ground turmeric

1 small egg, beaten

2 tbsp rice flour

corn oil, for deep-frying

fresh red chilies, to garnish

TO SERVE

cucumber slices

chili dipping sauce

1 Using a small, sharp knife, cut around the end of the bone at the cut end of each wing, then loosen the flesh away from around the bone, scraping it downward with the knife and pulling back the skin as you go. When you reach the next joint, grasp the end of the bone and twist sharply to break it at the joint. Remove the bone and turn back the flesh.

2 Continue to scrape the meat away down the length of the next long bone, exposing the joint. Twist to break the bone at the joint and remove, leaving just the wing tip in place.

3 Meanwhile, soak the dried shrimp in the hot water for 10–15 minutes. Drain, then chop. Place the pork, shrimp, garlic, fish sauce, salt, and pepper in a food processor and process to a smooth paste. Transfer to a bowl and add the scallions. Stir well. Use the mixture to stuff the chicken wings, pressing it down inside with your finger.

4 Beat the turmeric into the beaten egg and reserve until required. Dip each wing into the rice flour, shaking off the excess.

5 Heat a 2-inch/5-cm depth of oil in a large, heavy-bottom pan to 350–375°F/180–190°C, or until a cube of bread browns in 30 seconds. Dip the floured chicken wings quickly into the beaten egg, then drop carefully into the hot oil and deep-fry in small batches for 8–10 minutes, turning them over once. Drain the chicken wings on paper towels. Garnish with chilies and serve with cucumber slices and a chili dipping sauce.

# chicken satay

## serves eight

2 lb/900 g chicken breast meat,
    cut into ¼-inch/5-mm thick,
    1-inch/2.5-cm wide strips

MARINADE

1 lemongrass stem (tender inner
    part only)

2 tbsp vegetable oil

2 tbsp soy sauce

2 tsp tamarind paste

2 garlic cloves, crushed

1 tsp ground cumin

1 tsp ground coriander

1 tbsp lime juice

1 tsp brown sugar

PEANUT SAUCE

2 tbsp smooth peanut butter

generous ¾ cup coconut cream

2 tsp Thai red curry paste

1 tbsp fish sauce

1 tbsp brown sugar

1 Thread the chicken on to presoaked bamboo skewers (see Cook's Tip, page 82).

2 To make the marinade, chop the lemongrass and place in a food processor with the oil, soy sauce, tamarind paste, garlic, cumin, coriander, lime juice, and sugar. Process to a paste. Transfer to a bowl.

3 Add the chicken to the marinade and toss to coat. Cover with plastic wrap and let marinate in the refrigerator for at least 1 hour.

4 Preheat the broiler to medium. Place the peanut butter, coconut cream, red curry paste, fish sauce, and sugar in a pan. Heat gently, stirring constantly, to form a smooth sauce.

5 Cook the chicken under the hot broiler for 3–5 minutes on each side, or until the chicken is cooked through. Alternatively, grill over medium–hot coals. Reheat the sauce, adding a little hot water if necessary, and serve with the chicken satay.

# hot chili relish with crudités

## serves four

RELISH

6 garlic cloves

8–10 large fresh red chilies, seeded

and finely chopped

½ cup water

½ tsp salt

2 tsp sugar

juice of 1 lime

1 tbsp Thai fish sauce

1 tbsp vegetable oil

CRUDITES

carrot sticks

radishes

cucumber batons

baby corn cobs

1 Finely chop the garlic and place in a preheated wok with the remaining relish ingredients. Bring to a boil, then cover and simmer for 10 minutes.

2 Transfer the mixture to a food processor and blend until smooth.

3 Prepare the vegetable crudités. Transfer the relish to a bowl and serve with the crudités.

# sticky ginger chicken wings

## serves four

2 garlic cloves, coarsely chopped

1 piece preserved ginger in syrup,
  coarsely chopped

1 tsp coriander seeds

2 tbsp preserved ginger syrup

2 tbsp dark soy sauce

1 tbsp lime juice

1 tsp sesame oil

12 chicken wings

TO GARNISH

lime wedges

cilantro leaves

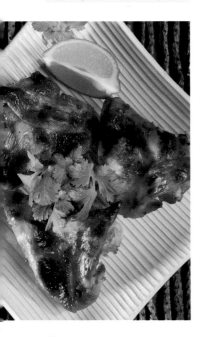

1 Place the garlic, preserved ginger, and coriander seeds in a mortar and, using a pestle, grind to a paste, gradually working in the ginger syrup, soy sauce, lime juice, and oil.

2 Tuck the pointed tip of each chicken wing underneath the thicker end of the wing to make a neat triangular shape. Place in a large bowl.

3 Add the garlic and ginger paste to the bowl and toss the chicken wings in the mixture to coat evenly. Cover with plastic wrap and let marinate in the refrigerator for several hours or overnight.

4 Preheat the broiler to medium. Arrange the chicken wings in a single layer on a foil-lined broiler pan and cook under the hot broiler for 12–15 minutes, turning them occasionally, until golden brown and thoroughly cooked.

5 Alternatively, cook on a lightly oiled grill rack over medium–hot coals. Transfer to individual serving plates and garnish with lime wedges and cilantro leaves, then serve immediately.

# chicken fried in banana leaves

## serves four–six

1 garlic clove, chopped

1 tsp finely chopped fresh
    gingerroot

¼ tsp pepper

2 cilantro sprigs

1 tbsp Thai fish sauce

1 tbsp whiskey

3 skinless, boneless chicken breasts

2–3 banana leaves, cut into 3-inch/
    7.5-cm squares

corn oil, for pan-frying

chili dipping sauce, to serve

### COOK'S TIP

To make a sweet chili dipping
sauce to serve with the chicken
pieces, mix equal amounts of
chili sauce and tomato ketchup
together, then stir in a dash of
rice wine to taste.

1 Place the garlic, ginger, pepper, cilantro sprigs, fish sauce, and whiskey in a mortar and, using a pestle, grind to a smooth paste.

2 Cut the chicken into 1-inch/ 2.5-cm chunks and toss in the paste to coat evenly. Cover and let marinate in the refrigerator for 1 hour.

3 Place a piece of chicken on a square of banana leaf and wrap it up like a package to enclose the chicken completely. Secure with wooden toothpicks or tie with a piece of string.

4 Heat an ⅛-inch/3-mm depth of oil for pan-frying in a large, heavy-bottom skillet until hot.

5 Pan-fry the packages for 8–10 minutes, turning them over occasionally, until golden brown and the chicken is thoroughly cooked. Serve with a chili dipping sauce.

# chicken balls with dipping sauce

### serves four–six

2 large skinless, boneless
    chicken breasts
3 tbsp vegetable oil
2 shallots, finely chopped
½ celery stalk, finely chopped
1 garlic clove, crushed
2 tbsp light soy sauce
1 small egg, lightly beaten
salt and pepper
1 bunch of scallions
DIPPING SAUCE
3 tbsp dark soy sauce
1 tbsp rice wine or dry sherry
1 tsp sesame seeds
scallion tassels, to garnish
    (see Cook's Tip, page 100)

1 Cut the chicken into ¾-inch/2-cm
pieces. Heat half the oil in a
large skillet. Add the chicken and stir-
fry over high heat for 2–3 minutes, or
until golden. Remove the chicken
with a slotted spoon and reserve
until required.

2 Add the shallots, celery, and
garlic to the skillet and stir-fry for
1–2 minutes, or until softened but
not browned.

3 Place the reserved chicken,
shallots, celery, and garlic in a
food processor and process until finely
ground. Add 1 tablespoon of
the light soy sauce, just enough egg
to make a fairly firm mixture, and salt
and pepper to taste.

4 Trim the scallions and cut into
2-inch/5-cm lengths. Reserve until
required. Make the dipping sauce by
mixing the dark soy sauce, rice wine,
and sesame seeds together in a small
bowl. Reserve.

5 Form the chicken mixture into
16–18 walnut-size balls between
the palms of your hands. Heat the
remaining oil in the skillet and then
stir-fry the balls in small batches for
4–5 minutes, or until golden brown.
As each batch is cooked, drain on
paper towels and keep hot.

6 Stir-fry the reserved scallions for
1–2 minutes, or until they begin
to soften, then stir in the remaining
light soy sauce. Serve with the chicken
balls and dipping sauce, garnished
with scallion tassels.

# spring rolls

## makes thirty

1 tbsp vegetable oil

2¼ cups lean ground pork

1 garlic clove, crushed

1 fresh red chili, seeded and
finely chopped

4 oz/115 g cooked, shelled shrimp

2 scallions, finely chopped

1-inch/2.5-cm piece fresh
gingerroot, finely grated

2 tbsp chopped cilantro

2 tsp Thai fish sauce

30 spring roll wrappers

corn oil, for deep-frying

sweet chili dipping sauce, to serve

1 Heat the vegetable oil in a
skillet. Add the pork, garlic, and
chili and cook, stirring, until the pork
is browned.

2 Chop the shrimp, then add to the
skillet with the scallions, ginger,
cilantro, and fish sauce. Cook, stirring,
until heated through. Remove the
skillet from the heat and let cool.

3 Prepare the spring roll
wrappers according to the
package directions.

4 Place a spoonful of the pork
mixture down the center of each
spring roll wrapper, leaving a space at
the top and bottom and down the
side. Brush the edges with water. Fold
the top and bottom over and then fold
in the sides to form a sealed roll.

5 Just before serving, heat the oil
for deep-frying in a large pan or
wok until nearly smoking. Deep-fry the
rolls in batches for 2–3 minutes, or
until golden brown. Drain on paper
towels and keep warm while cooking
the remainder. Serve with a sweet chili
dipping sauce.

# stuffed eggs with pork & crabmeat

## serves four

4 large eggs

scant 1 cup ground pork

6 oz/175 g canned white
   crabmeat, drained

1 garlic clove, crushed

1 tsp Thai fish sauce

½ tsp ground lemongrass

1 tbsp chopped cilantro

1 tbsp dry unsweetened coconut

salt and pepper

⅔ cup all-purpose flour

about ⅔ cup coconut milk

corn oil, for deep-frying

cucumber flowers, to garnish

green salad, to serve

1 Place the eggs in a pan of simmering water and bring to a boil, then let simmer for 10 minutes. Drain the eggs, then crack the shells and cool under cold running water. Peel off the shells.

2 Cut the eggs lengthwise down the center and scoop out the yolks. Place the yolks in a bowl with the pork, crabmeat, garlic, fish sauce, lemongrass, cilantro, and coconut. Season to taste with salt and pepper and mix well.

3 Divide the mixture into 8 equal-size portions, then fill each of the egg whites with the mixture, pressing together with your hands to form the shape of a whole egg.

4 Whisk the flour and enough coconut milk together to form a thick batter. Season to taste.

5 Heat a 2-inch/5-cm depth of oil in a large, heavy-bottom pan to 350–375°F/180–190°C, or until a cube of bread browns in 30 seconds. Dip each egg into the coconut batter, then shake off the excess.

6 Deep-fry the eggs in batches for 5 minutes, turning occasionally, until golden brown. Remove with a slotted spoon and drain on paper towels. Transfer to plates, then garnish with cucumber flowers and serve with a green salad.

3

2

5

# pork appetizer in lettuce cups

## serves six

2 fresh red chilies

4 garlic cloves, finely chopped

1 tbsp chopped cilantro root

1 tbsp grated fresh gingerroot

3 tbsp vegetable oil

1 tbsp hot water

1 lb 2 oz/500 g ground lean pork

2 fresh kaffir lime leaves,
   finely shredded

2 tbsp Thai fish sauce

1 tsp brown sugar

2 tbsp coarsely chopped cilantro

12 leaves romaine lettuce or similar
   firm lettuce leaves (see Cook's
   Tip, page 194)

TO GARNISH

cilantro leaves

thin strips of fresh red chili

1 Seed and finely chop the chilies, then place in a food processor with the garlic, cilantro root, ginger, oil, and water. Process until smooth.

2 Transfer to a preheated wok or large skillet.

3 Stir-fry the paste for 4 minutes over medium heat, then increase the heat and add the pork. Stir-fry for 3 minutes, or until colored.

4 Add the lime leaves, fish sauce, sugar, and chopped cilantro. Continue to stir-fry until the pork is dry.

5 Arrange the pork in lettuce cups, then garnish with cilantro leaves and strips of chili and serve.

57

# pork-stuffed omelet

## serves four

2 garlic cloves, chopped

4 black peppercorns

4 cilantro sprigs

2 tbsp vegetable oil

1¾ cups ground pork

2 scallions, chopped

1 large firm tomato, chopped

6 large eggs

1 tbsp Thai fish sauce

¼ tsp ground turmeric

mixed salad greens, tossed, to serve

1 Place the garlic, peppercorns, and cilantro in a mortar and, using a pestle, grind to a smooth paste.

2 Heat 1 tablespoon of the oil in a large skillet. Add the paste and stir-fry for 1–2 minutes, or until it just changes color.

3 Stir in the pork and stir-fry until it is lightly browned. Add the scallions and tomato, and stir-fry for an additional 1 minute, then remove the skillet from the heat.

4 Heat the remaining oil in a small, heavy-bottom skillet. Beat the eggs with the fish sauce and turmeric, then pour one-fourth of the egg mixture into the skillet. As the mixture begins to set, stir lightly to ensure that all the liquid egg is set.

5 Spoon one-fourth of the pork mixture down the center of the omelet, then fold the sides inward toward the center, enclosing the filling. Transfer to a heatproof plate and keep warm. Make 3 more omelets with the remaining egg and fill with the remaining pork mixture.

6 Slide the omelets on to serving plates and serve with salad.

# vegetarian spring rolls

### serves four

1 oz/25 g fine cellophane noodles

2 tbsp peanut oil, plus extra for
　deep-frying

2 garlic cloves, crushed

½ tsp grated fresh gingerroot

1 cup thinly sliced oyster
　mushrooms

2 scallions, finely chopped

½ cup fresh bean sprouts

1 small carrot, finely shredded

½ tsp sesame oil

1 tbsp light soy sauce

1 tbsp rice wine or dry sherry

¼ tsp pepper

1 tbsp chopped cilantro

1 tbsp chopped fresh mint

24 spring roll wrappers

½ tsp cornstarch

1 fresh mint sprig, to garnish

chili dipping sauce, to serve

1 Place the noodles in a heatproof bowl, then pour over enough boiling water to cover and let stand for 4 minutes. Drain and rinse in cold water, then drain again. Use a sharp knife to cut into 2-inch/5-cm lengths.

2 Heat the peanut oil in a preheated wok or wide skillet. Add the garlic, ginger, mushrooms, scallions, bean sprouts, and carrot and stir-fry for 1 minute, or until soft.

3 Stir in the sesame oil, soy sauce, rice wine, pepper, cilantro, and mint, then remove the wok from the heat. Stir in the noodles.

4 Arrange the spring roll wrappers on a counter, pointing diagonally. Mix the cornstarch with a little water and use to brush the edges of a wrapper. Spoon some filling on to the pointed side of the same wrapper.

5 Roll the point of the wrapper over the filling, then fold the side points inward over the filling. Continue to roll up the wrapper away from you, moistening the tip with more cornstarch mixture to secure the roll. Make up all the spring rolls in the same way.

6 Heat the oil for deep-frying in a wok or deep skillet to 350–375°F/180–190°C, or until a cube of bread browns in 30 seconds. Deep-fry the rolls in batches for 2–3 minutes each, or until golden brown and crisp. Drain and transfer to a plate. Garnish with a mint sprig and serve with a chili dipping sauce.

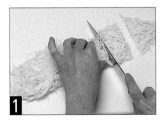

# tuna & tomato salad with ginger dressing

## serves four

½ cup shredded Napa cabbage

3 tbsp rice wine or dry sherry

2 tbsp Thai fish sauce

1 tbsp finely shredded fresh
   gingerroot

1 garlic clove, finely chopped

½ small fresh red Thai chili,
   finely chopped

2 tsp brown sugar

2 tbsp lime juice

14 oz/400 g fresh tuna steak

corn oil, for brushing

4½ oz/125 g cherry tomatoes

fresh mint leaves and mint sprigs,
   coarsely chopped, to garnish

### COOK'S TIP

The dressing can be made in
advance and spooned over the
dish just before serving.

1 Place a small pile of shredded Napa cabbage on a large serving plate. Place the rice wine, fish sauce, ginger, garlic, chili, sugar, and 1 tablespoon of lime juice in a screw-top jar and shake well to combine.

2 Using a sharp knife, cut the tuna into strips of an even thickness. Sprinkle with the remaining lime juice.

3 Brush a wide skillet or ridged grill pan with oil and heat until very hot. Arrange the tuna strips in the skillet and cook until just firm and light golden, turning them over once. Remove the tuna strips from the skillet and reserve.

4 Add the tomatoes to the skillet and cook over high heat until lightly browned. Spoon the tuna and tomatoes over the Napa cabbage, then spoon over the dressing. Garnish with fresh mint and serve warm.

# sweet & sour seafood salad

### serves six

18 live mussels in shells

6 large scallops, shelled

7 oz/200 g baby squid, cleaned

2 shallots, finely chopped

6 raw jumbo shrimp, shelled
  and deveined

¼ cucumber

1 carrot

¼ head Napa cabbage, shredded

DRESSING

4 tbsp lime juice

2 garlic cloves, finely chopped

2 tbsp Thai fish sauce

1 tsp sesame oil

1 tbsp brown sugar

2 tbsp chopped fresh mint

½ tsp pepper

salt

1 Clean the mussels by scrubbing or scraping the shells and pulling out any beards that are attached to them. Discard any with broken shells or any that refuse to close when tapped. Place the mussels in a large pan with just the water that clings to their shells and cook, covered, over high heat for 3–4 minutes, shaking the pan occasionally, until they have opened. Remove the mussels with a slotted spoon, reserving the liquid in the pan. Discard any mussels that remain closed.

2 Using a sharp knife, separate the corals from the scallops, then cut the white parts in half horizontally. Cut the tentacles from the squid and slice the body cavities into rings.

3 Add the shallots to the liquid in the pan and simmer over high heat until the liquid is reduced to 3 tablespoons. Add the scallops, squid, and jumbo shrimp and stir for 2–3 minutes, or until cooked. Remove the pan from the heat and transfer the mixture to a wide bowl. Add the mussels.

4 Cut the cucumber and carrot in half lengthwise, then slice thinly on a diagonal angle to make long, pointed slices. Toss with the Napa cabbage. To make the dressing, place all the ingredients in a screw-top jar and shake well until evenly combined. Season to taste with salt.

5 Add the vegetables to the seafood in the bowl and toss together. Spoon the dressing over and serve immediately.

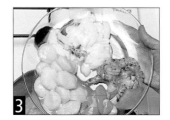

# Fish & Seafood

The Thais are primarily a fish-eating nation, with meat often being reserved for special celebrations. The waterways of Thailand are teeming with many types of fish—even in the channels between the paddy fields—and the warm seas bring an abundance of fish and shellfish.

Even in the heart of Bangkok city, the markets are packed with fresh fish and seafood of all kinds. In Thai coastal towns, rows of thatch-roofed beach kiosks sell every type of fresh seafood from the warm Gulf waters—from grilled or sautéed fish with ginger, to shrimp in coconut milk and cilantro—to locals and visitors alike.

# steamed yellow fish fillets

## serves four

1 lb 2 oz/500 g firm fish fillets, such
    as red snapper, sole, or angler fish

1 red bird chili

1 small onion, chopped

3 garlic cloves, chopped

2 cilantro sprigs

1 tsp coriander seeds

½ tsp ground turmeric

½ tsp pepper

1 tbsp Thai fish sauce

2 tbsp coconut milk

1 small egg, beaten

2 tbsp rice flour

fresh red and green chili strips,
    to garnish

stir-fried vegetables, to serve

1 Using a sharp knife, remove any skin from the fish and cut the fillets diagonally into ¾-inch/2-cm wide strips.

2 Place the bird chili, onion, garlic, cilantro, and coriander seeds in a mortar and, using a pestle, grind to a smooth paste.

3 Transfer the paste to a bowl and add the turmeric, pepper, fish sauce, coconut milk, and beaten egg, stirring to mix evenly. Spread the rice flour out on a large plate. Dip the fish strips into the paste mixture, then into the rice flour to coat lightly.

4 Bring the water in the bottom of a steamer to a boil, then arrange the fish strips in the top of the steamer. Cover and steam for 12–15 minutes, or until the fish is just firm.

5 Garnish the fish with the chili strips and serve immediately with stir-fried vegetables.

# fish curry

## serves four

4 shallots, coarsely chopped

2-inch/5-cm piece fresh gingerroot,
 finely sliced

2-inch/5-cm piece lemongrass,
 outer leaves discarded

2-inch/5-cm piece fresh galangal,
 finely chopped

3 fresh red chilies, seeded and
 coarsely chopped

1 tbsp ground almonds

½ tsp ground turmeric

½ tsp salt

1¾ cups coconut cream

4 fish steaks, such as cod, turbot,
 or halibut

TO GARNISH

1 fresh red chili, cut into thin strips

2 tbsp toasted slivered almonds

salad, to serve

1 Coarsely chop the shallots and place in a food processor with the ginger, lemongrass, galangal, chilies, ground almonds, turmeric, and salt. Add 6 tablespoons of the coconut cream and process to a smooth paste.

2 Pour the paste into a large pan. Bring to a boil and cook, stirring constantly, for 4 minutes. Add the remaining coconut cream and return to a boil.

3 Place the fish steaks in the pan and let simmer for 10 minutes, turning once, until the fish is cooked and flakes easily when tested with a fork. If the sauce is too thin, transfer the fish to a warmed serving dish and boil the sauce to reduce to the desired consistency. Garnish with chili strips and toasted slivered almonds and serve with a salad of your choice.

# baked fish with bell pepper, chilies & basil

## serves four

handful of fresh basil leaves

1 lb 10 oz/750 g whole red
  snapper, sea bass, or tilapia,
  cleaned

2 tbsp peanut oil

2 tbsp Thai fish sauce

2 garlic cloves, crushed

1 tsp finely grated fresh gingerroot
  or galangal

2 large fresh red chilies,
  diagonally sliced

1 yellow bell pepper, seeded
  and diced

1 tbsp palm sugar

1 tbsp rice vinegar or white
  wine vinegar

2 tbsp water or fish stock

2 tomatoes, seeded and sliced into
  thin wedges

mixed salad, to serve

### COOK'S TIP

Almost any whole fish can be
cooked by this method, but
snapper, sea bass, or tilapia are
particularly good with the
Thai flavors.

1 Preheat the oven to 375°F/190°C. Reserve a few basil leaves for the garnish and tuck the rest inside the body cavity of the fish.

2 Heat 1 tablespoon of the oil in a wide skillet. Add the fish and cook quickly to brown, turning once. Place the fish on a large piece of foil in a roasting pan and spoon over the fish sauce. Wrap the foil over the fish loosely and bake in the preheated oven for 25–30 minutes, or until just cooked through.

3 Meanwhile, heat the remaining oil in a clean skillet. Add the garlic, ginger, and chilies and cook for 30 seconds. Add the bell pepper and stir-fry for an additional 2–3 minutes to soften.

4 Stir in the sugar, rice vinegar, and water, then add the tomatoes and bring to a boil. Remove the skillet from the heat.

5 Remove the fish from the oven and transfer to a warmed serving plate. Add the fish juices to the skillet, then spoon the sauce over the fish. Sprinkle with the reserved basil leaves and serve immediately with a salad.

# curried mussel soup

1 tsp coriander seeds

1 tsp cumin seeds

2 lb/900 g live mussels in shells

scant ½ cup white wine

scant ¼ cup butter

1 onion, finely chopped

1 garlic clove, finely chopped

1 tsp grated fresh gingerroot

1 tsp ground turmeric

pinch of cayenne pepper

2½ cups fish stock

4 tbsp heavy cream

2 tbsp all-purpose flour

2 tbsp chopped cilantro,
   to garnish

1 Cook the coriander and cumin seeds in a dry skillet until they begin to smell aromatic and start to pop. Transfer to a mortar and, using a pestle, grind to a powder. Reserve.

2 Clean the mussels by scrubbing or scraping the shells and pulling out any beards that are attached to them. Discard any with broken shells or any that refuse to close when tapped. Place the mussels in a large pan with the wine and cook, covered, over high heat for 3–4 minutes, shaking the pan occasionally, until the mussels have opened. Discard any mussels that remain closed. Drain, reserving the cooking liquid, and let the mussels stand until cool enough to handle. Remove two-thirds of the mussels from their shells and set them all aside. Pour the mussel cooking liquid through a strainer and reserve.

3 Heat half the butter in a large pan. Add the onion and cook gently for 4–5 minutes, or until softened but not colored. Add the garlic and ginger and cook for an additional 1 minute before adding the roasted and ground spices, the turmeric, and cayenne. Cook for 1 minute before adding the stock, reserved mussel cooking liquid, and cream. Simmer for 10 minutes.

4 Cream the remaining butter and flour together to a thick paste. Add the paste to the simmering soup and stir until dissolved and the soup has thickened slightly. Add the mussels and heat gently for 2 minutes. Garnish with cilantro and serve.

# fish cakes with sweet & sour dip

## serves four

1 lb/450 g firm white fish, skinned
   and coarsely chopped

1 tbsp Thai fish sauce

1 tbsp Thai red curry paste

1 fresh kaffir lime leaf, shredded

2 tbsp chopped cilantro

1 egg

1 tsp brown sugar

large pinch of salt

⅓ cup green beans, thinly sliced
   crosswise

vegetable oil, for pan-frying

SWEET & SOUR DIP

4 tbsp sugar

1 tbsp cold water

3 tbsp white rice vinegar

2 small fresh chilies, finely chopped

1 tbsp Thai fish sauce

TO GARNISH

scallion tassels (see page 100)

fresh red chili flowers
   (see page 160)

### COOK'S TIP

It isn't necessary to use the most
expensive cut of white fish in this
recipe because the other flavors
are very strong.

1 To make the fish cakes, place the fish, fish sauce, curry paste, lime leaf, cilantro, egg, brown sugar, and salt in a food processor and process until smooth. Scrape into a bowl and stir in the green beans. Reserve.

2 To make the dipping sauce, place the sugar, water, and rice vinegar in a small pan and heat gently until the sugar has dissolved. Bring to a boil, then reduce the heat and simmer for 2 minutes. Remove the pan from the heat and stir in the chilies and fish sauce. Let cool until required.

3 Heat a skillet with enough oil to cover the bottom generously. Divide the fish mixture into 16 balls. Flatten the balls into patties and cook in the oil for 1–2 minutes on each side until golden. Drain on paper towels. Garnish with scallion tassels and chili flowers and serve with the dip.

# whole fried fish with soy & ginger

## serves four–six

6 dried shiitake mushrooms

3 tbsp rice vinegar

2 tbsp brown sugar

3 tbsp dark soy sauce

3-inch/7.5-cm piece fresh
    gingerroot, finely chopped

4 scallions, diagonally sliced

2 tsp cornstarch

2 tbsp lime juice

1 sea bass, about 2 lb 4 oz/
    1 kg, cleaned

salt and pepper

4 tbsp all-purpose flour

corn oil, for frying

1 radish, sliced but left whole,
    to garnish

TO SERVE

shredded Napa cabbage

radish slices

### COOK'S TIP

Buy a very fresh whole fish on
the day you plan to cook it, and
ask your fish dealer to clean it,
preferably leaving the head on.

1 Place the dried mushrooms in a bowl, then cover with hot water and let soak for 10 minutes. Drain well, reserving a scant ½ cup of the liquid. Using a sharp knife, cut the mushrooms into thin slices.

2 Mix the reserved mushroom liquid with the rice vinegar, sugar, and soy sauce. Place in a pan with the mushrooms and bring to a boil. Reduce the heat and simmer for 3–4 minutes.

3 Add the ginger and scallions and simmer for 1 minute. Blend the cornstarch and lime juice together, then add to the pan and stir for 1–2 minutes, or until the sauce thickens and clears. Reserve until required.

4 Season the fish inside and out, then dust lightly with flour, carefully shaking off the excess.

5 Heat a 1-inch/2.5-cm depth of oil in a wide skillet to 350–375°F/ 180–190°C, or until a cube of bread browns in 30 seconds. Lower the fish into the oil and cook on one side for 3–4 minutes, or until golden. Use 2 metal spatulas to turn the fish and cook on the other side for an additional 3–4 minutes, or until golden brown.

6 Lift the fish out of the skillet, draining off the excess oil, and place on a serving plate. Heat the reserved sauce until boiling, then spoon it over the fish. Serve immediately with Napa cabbage and radish slices, garnished with the sliced radish.

# baked cod with a curry crust

## serves four

½ tsp sesame oil

4 cod fillet pieces, about

    5½ oz/150 g each

1½ cups fresh white bread crumbs

2 tbsp blanched almonds, chopped

2 tsp Thai green curry paste

finely grated rind of ½ lime, plus

    extra thinly pared rind to garnish

salt and pepper

lime slices, to garnish

TO SERVE

boiled new potatoes

mixed salad greens

1 Preheat the oven to 400°F/200°C. Brush the oil over the bottom of a wide, shallow ovenproof dish or pan, then arrange the cod pieces in a single layer.

2 Mix the bread crumbs, almonds, curry paste, and grated lime rind together in a bowl, stirring well to blend thoroughly and evenly. Season to taste with salt and pepper.

3 Carefully spoon the crumb mixture over the fish pieces, pressing lightly with your hand to hold it in place.

4 Bake the dish, uncovered, in the preheated oven for 35–40 minutes, or until the fish is cooked through and the crumb topping is golden brown.

5 Serve the dish hot, garnished with lime slices and rind and accompanied by boiled new potatoes and mixed salad greens.

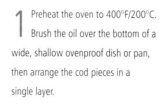

### COOK'S TIP

To test whether the fish is cooked through, use a fork to pierce it in the thickest part—if the flesh is white all the way through and flakes apart easily, it is cooked sufficiently.

# spicy thai seafood stew

## serves four

7 oz/200 g squid, cleaned and
   tentacles discarded
1 lb 2 oz/500 g firm white fish fillet,
   preferably angler fish or halibut
1 tbsp corn oil
4 shallots, finely chopped
2 garlic cloves, finely chopped
2 tbsp Thai green curry paste
2 small lemongrass stems,
   finely chopped
1 tsp shrimp paste
generous 2 cups coconut milk
7 oz/200 g raw jumbo shrimp,
   shelled and deveined
12 live clams in shells, cleaned
8 fresh basil leaves, finely shredded
fresh basil leaves, to garnish
freshly cooked rice, to serve

1 Using a sharp knife, cut the squid body cavities into thick rings and the white fish into bite-size chunks.

2 Heat the oil in a large skillet or preheated wok. Add the shallots, garlic, and curry paste and stir-fry for 1–2 minutes. Add the lemongrass and shrimp paste, then stir in the coconut milk and bring to a boil.

3 Reduce the heat until the liquid is simmering gently, then add the white fish, squid, and shrimp to the skillet and simmer for 2 minutes.

4 Add the clams and simmer for an additional 1 minute, or until the clams have opened. Discard any clams that remain closed.

5 Sprinkle the shredded basil leaves over the stew. Transfer to serving plates, then garnish with whole basil leaves and serve immediately with rice.

## VARIATION

If you prefer, live mussels in shells can be used instead of clams—add them after the shrimp and continue as in the recipe.

# spiced steamed fish

## serves four–six

1-inch/2.5-cm piece fresh
   gingerroot, finely grated
1 lemongrass stem (base only),
   thinly sliced
6 fresh red chilies, seeded and
   coarsely chopped
1 small red onion, finely chopped
1 tbsp Thai fish sauce
2 lb/900 g whole fish, cleaned
2 fresh kaffir lime leaves,
   thinly sliced
2 fresh basil sprigs
TO SERVE
freshly cooked rice
cucumber, cut into thin sticks

1 Place the ginger, lemongrass, chilies, onion, and fish sauce in a food processor. Process to a coarse paste, adding a little water, if needed.

2 Cut 3–4 deep slits crosswise on each side of the fish. Spread over the spice paste, rubbing it well into the slits. Place the fish in a dish deep enough to hold the liquid that collects during steaming. Sprinkle over the lime leaves and basil.

3 Set up a steamer or place a rack into a wok or deep pan. Bring about 2 inches/5 cm of water to a boil in the steamer or wok.

4 Place the dish of fish into the steamer or on to the rack. Reduce the heat to a simmer, then cover tightly and steam the fish for 15–20 minutes, or until the fish is cooked through. Serve with freshly cooked rice and cucumber sticks.

**COOK'S TIP**
You can use any whole fish in this recipe, such as sea bass, red snapper, trout, or tilapia.

# pan-fried spiced salmon

## serves four

1-inch/2.5-cm piece fresh
   gingerroot, grated

1 tsp coriander seeds, crushed

¼ tsp chili powder

1 tbsp lime juice

1 tsp sesame oil

4 salmon fillet pieces with skin,
   about 5½ oz/150 g each

2 tbsp vegetable oil

cilantro leaves, to garnish

TO SERVE

freshly cooked rice

stir-fried vegetables

1 Mix the ginger, crushed coriander, chili powder, lime juice, and sesame oil together in a bowl.

2 Place the salmon on a wide, nonmetallic plate or dish and spoon the mixture over the flesh side of the fillets, spreading it to coat each piece of salmon evenly.

3 Cover the dish with plastic wrap and let chill in the refrigerator for 30 minutes.

4 Heat a wide, heavy-bottom skillet or ridged grill pan with the vegetable oil over high heat. Place the salmon in the hot skillet, skin-side down, and cook for 4–5 minutes, without turning, until the salmon is crusty underneath and the flesh flakes easily.

5 Serve the salmon immediately, with freshly cooked rice, garnished with cilantro leaves, and stir-fried vegetables.

### COOK'S TIP

Use a heavy-bottom skillet
or solid grill pan to ensure that
the fish cooks evenly throughout
without sticking. If the fish is
very thick, you may prefer to turn
it over to cook on the other side
for 2–3 minutes.

# spiced tuna in sweet & sour sauce

## serves four

4 fresh tuna steaks, about 1 lb 2 oz/
   500 g in total

¼ tsp pepper

2 tbsp peanut oil

1 onion, diced

1 small red bell pepper, seeded and
   cut into short thin sticks

1 garlic clove, crushed

½ cucumber, seeded and cut
   into short thin sticks

2 pineapple slices, diced

1 tsp finely chopped fresh
   gingerroot

1 tbsp brown sugar

1 tbsp cornstarch

1½ tbsp lime juice

1 tbsp Thai fish sauce

1 cup fish stock

TO GARNISH

lime slices

cucumber slices

### COOK'S TIP

Tuna can be served quite
lightly cooked. It can be dry
if overcooked.

1 Sprinkle the tuna steaks with pepper on both sides. Heat a heavy-bottom skillet or ridged grill pan and brush with a little of the oil. Arrange the tuna steaks in the skillet and cook for 8 minutes, turning them over once.

2 Meanwhile, heat the remaining oil in a separate skillet. Add the onion, bell pepper, and garlic and cook gently for 3–4 minutes to soften.

3 Remove the skillet from the heat and stir in the cucumber, pineapple, ginger, and sugar.

4 Blend the cornstarch with the lime juice and fish sauce, then stir into the stock and add to the skillet. Stir over medium heat until boiling, then cook for 1–2 minutes, or until thickened and clear.

5 Spoon the sauce over the tuna and serve immediately, garnished with slices of lime and cucumber.

# salmon with red curry in banana leaves

## serves four

4 salmon steaks, about
   6 oz/175 g each
2 banana leaves, halved
1 garlic clove, crushed
1 tsp grated fresh gingerroot
1 tbsp Thai red curry paste
1 tsp brown sugar
1 tbsp Thai fish sauce
2 tbsp lime juice
TO GARNISH
lime wedges
whole fresh red chilies
finely chopped fresh red chili

1 Preheat the oven to 425°F/220°C. Place a salmon steak in the center of each half banana leaf.

2 Mix the garlic, ginger, curry paste, sugar, and fish sauce together, then spread over the surface of the fish. Sprinkle with lime juice.

3 Carefully wrap the banana leaves around the fish, tucking in the sides as you go to make neat, compact pockets.

4 Place the pockets seam-side down on a baking sheet. Bake in the preheated oven for 15–20 minutes, or until the fish is cooked and the banana leaves are beginning to brown. Serve garnished with lime wedges, whole chilies, and finely chopped chili.

### COOK'S TIP

Fresh banana leaves are often sold in packages containing several leaves, but if you buy more than you need, they will store in the refrigerator for about a week.

# coconut shrimp

## serves four

½ cup dry unsweetened coconut

½ cup fresh white bread crumbs

1 tsp Chinese five-spice powder

½ tsp salt

finely grated rind of 1 lime

1 egg white

1 lb/450 g raw fantail shrimp

corn oil, for frying

lemon wedges, to garnish

1 Mix the dry unsweetened coconut, bread crumbs, Chinese five-spice powder, salt, and lime rind together in a bowl.

2 Lightly whisk the egg white in a separate bowl.

3 Rinse the shrimp under cold running water and pat dry with paper towels.

4 Dip the shrimp into the egg white, then into the coconut crumb mixture, so that they are evenly coated.

5 Heat about 2 inches/5 cm of oil in a large, preheated wok.

6 Add the shrimp to the wok and stir-fry for 5 minutes, or until golden and crispy.

7 Remove the shrimp with a slotted spoon, then transfer to paper towels and let drain thoroughly.

8 Transfer the coconut shrimp to warmed serving dishes and garnish with lemon wedges. Serve immediately.

# shrimp skewers with tamarind glaze

## serves four

1 garlic clove, chopped

1 fresh red Thai chili, seeded
and chopped

1 tbsp tamarind paste

1 tbsp sesame oil

1 tbsp dark soy sauce

2 tbsp lime juice

1 tbsp brown sugar

16 large raw jumbo shrimp in shells

lime wedges, to garnish

TO SERVE

crusty bread

salad greens

### COOK'S TIP

Before using wooden or bamboo
skewers, soak them in water for
at least 30 minutes to prevent
them burning under the broiler.

1 Place the garlic, chili, tamarind
paste, sesame oil, soy sauce,
lime juice, and sugar in a small pan.
Stir constantly over low heat until the
sugar is dissolved, then remove the
pan from the heat and let cool
completely.

2 Rinse the shrimp under cold
running water and pat dry with
paper towels. Arrange in a single layer
in a wide, nonmetallic dish. Spoon the
marinade over the shrimp and turn to
coat evenly. Cover and let marinate in
the refrigerator for at least 2 hours or
preferably overnight.

3 Preheat the broiler to medium.
Thread 4 shrimp on to each
presoaked skewer and cook under the
preheated broiler for 5–6 minutes,
turning them over once, until they turn
pink and begin to brown. Alternatively,
grill over hot coals.

4 Thread a wedge of lime on to the
end of each skewer and serve
with crusty bread and salad greens.

# stir-fried squid with hot black bean sauce

## serves four

1 lb 10 oz/750 g squid, cleaned and
   tentacles discarded

1 large red bell pepper, seeded

scant 1 cup snow peas

1 head bok choy

3 tbsp black bean sauce

1 tbsp Thai fish sauce

1 tbsp rice wine or dry sherry

1 tbsp dark soy sauce

1 tsp brown sugar

1 tsp cornstarch

1 tbsp water

1 tbsp corn oil

1 tsp sesame oil

1 small fresh red Thai chili,
   chopped

1 garlic clove, finely chopped

1 tsp grated fresh gingerroot

2 scallions, chopped

### COOK'S TIP

Quick stir-frying is an ideal
cooking method for squid,
because if overcooked it can
be tough. It also seals in the
colors, flavors, and nutritional
value of fresh vegetables.

1 Cut the squid body cavities into fourths lengthwise. Use the tip of a small, sharp knife to score a diamond pattern into the flesh, without cutting all the way through. Pat dry with paper towels.

2 Cut the bell pepper into long, thin slices. Cut the snow peas in half diagonally. Coarsely shred the bok choy.

3 Mix the black bean sauce, fish sauce, rice wine, soy sauce, and sugar together in a bowl. Blend the cornstarch with the water and stir into the other sauce ingredients. Reserve until required.

4 Heat the oils in a preheated wok. Add the chili, garlic, ginger, and scallions and stir-fry for 1 minute. Add the bell pepper slices and stir-fry for 2 minutes.

5 Add the squid and stir-fry over high heat for an additional 1 minute. Stir in the snow peas and bok choy and stir for an additional 1 minute, or until wilted.

6 Stir in the sauce ingredients and cook, stirring constantly, for 2 minutes, or until the sauce thickens and clears. Serve immediately.

# spicy scallops with lime & chili

## serves four

16 large scallops, shelled

1 tbsp butter

1 tbsp vegetable oil

1 tsp crushed garlic

1 tsp grated fresh gingerroot

1 bunch of scallions,
   finely sliced

finely grated rind of 1 lime

1 small fresh red chili, seeded and
   very finely chopped

3 tbsp lime juice

lime wedges, to garnish

freshly cooked rice, to serve

1 Using a sharp knife, trim the scallops to remove any black intestine, then wash and pat dry with paper towels. Separate the corals from the white parts, then slice each white part in half horizontally, making 2 circles.

2 Heat the butter and oil in a skillet or preheated wok. Add the garlic and ginger and stir-fry for 1 minute without browning. Add the scallions and stir-fry for an additional 1 minute.

3 Add the scallops and continue stir-frying over high heat for 4–5 minutes. Stir in the lime rind, chili, and lime juice and cook for an additional 1 minute.

4 Transfer the scallops to serving plates, then spoon over the pan juices and garnish with lime wedges. Serve hot with freshly cooked rice.

# shrimp & pineapple curry

## serves four

½ fresh pineapple

1¾ cups coconut cream

2 tbsp Thai red curry paste

2 tbsp fish sauce

2 tsp sugar

12 oz/350 g raw jumbo shrimp

2 tbsp chopped cilantro

steamed jasmine rice, to serve

### VARIATION

For an extra touch, shred 4 scallions and sprinkle over just before serving.

1 Peel the pineapple and chop the flesh. Heat the coconut cream, pineapple, curry paste, fish sauce, and sugar until almost boiling.

2 Shell and devein the shrimp. Add the shrimp and cilantro to the pan and simmer for 3 minutes, or until the shrimp are cooked.

3 Serve the shrimp with steamed jasmine rice.

# Meat & Poultry

Because of the Thai Buddhist religion, which forbids the killing of animals, most butchers are immigrant workers in Thailand. Religion does not forbid eating meat, though it is often regarded as a special treat. Chicken is much more common than beef, and it's not unusual to see chicken, or sometimes pork, combined with seafood such as shrimp or crabmeat—a combination which works surprisingly well. Duck, another Thai favorite, is frequently grill-roasted with warm spices and soy or sweet glazes, much as in the customary Chinese style.

# beef & bell peppers with lemongrass

## serves four

## serves four

1 lb 2 oz/500 g lean beef fillet

2 tbsp vegetable oil

1 garlic clove, finely chopped

1 lemongrass stem, finely shredded

1-inch/2.5-cm piece fresh
   gingerroot, finely chopped

1 red bell pepper, seeded and
   thickly sliced

1 green bell pepper, seeded and
   thickly sliced

1 onion, thickly sliced

2 tbsp lime juice

salt and pepper

freshly cooked noodles or rice,
   to serve

3 Add the beef and stir-fry for an additional 2–3 minutes, or until lightly colored. Stir in the lemongrass and ginger and remove the skillet from the heat.

1 Cut the beef into long, thin strips, cutting across the grain.

2 Heat the oil in a large skillet or preheated wok over high heat. Add the garlic and stir-fry for 1 minute.

4 Remove the beef from the skillet and reserve to one side. Add the bell peppers and onion to the skillet and stir-fry over high heat for 2–3 minutes, or until the onions are just turning golden brown and slightly softened.

5 Return the beef to the skillet, then stir in the lime juice and season to taste with salt and pepper. Serve with freshly cooked noodles or rice.

# beef & coconut curry

## serves four

1 lb 12 oz/800 g braising steak

3 tbsp vegetable oil

2 onions, thinly sliced

2 tbsp Thai red curry paste

1 tbsp tamarind paste or lime juice

2 tbsp Thai fish sauce

3¾ cups coconut milk

2 tsp sugar

6 cardamom pods, crushed

1 small pineapple, peeled
    and chopped

TO SERVE

freshly cooked rice

shrimp chips

3 Stir in the tamarind paste, fish sauce, coconut milk, and sugar. Bring to a boil, then reduce the heat and return the beef and onions to the casserole with the cardamom.

4 Simmer gently, uncovered, for 1–1½ hours, or until the beef is tender. Stir from time to time, and if it is becoming dry, cover with a lid.

5 Add the pineapple and cook for an additional 5 minutes. The curry should be quite dry, but add a little water if necessary.

6 Serve immediately with rice and shrimp chips.

1 Cut the beef into cubes. Heat the oil in a flameproof casserole. Brown the beef in batches and reserve.

2 Add the onions to the oil and cook for 5 minutes, then reserve with the beef. Add the curry paste and cook gently for 1 minute, stirring constantly.

# stir-fried beef with bean sprouts

## serves four

1 bunch of scallions

2 tbsp corn oil

1 garlic clove, crushed

1 tsp finely chopped fresh
  gingerroot

1 lb 2 oz/500 g lean beef fillet, cut
  into thin strips

1 large red bell pepper, seeded
  and sliced

1 small fresh red chili, seeded
  and chopped

3 cups fresh bean sprouts

1 small lemongrass stem,
  finely chopped

2 tbsp smooth peanut butter

4 tbsp coconut milk

1 tbsp rice vinegar or white
  wine vinegar

1 tbsp soy sauce

1 tsp brown sugar

9 oz/250 g medium egg noodles

salt and pepper

1 Thinly slice the scallions,
reserving some slices to use as
a garnish.

2 Heat the oil in a skillet or
preheated wok over high heat.
Add the scallions, garlic, and ginger
and stir-fry for 2–3 minutes to soften.
Add the beef and continue stir-frying
for 4–5 minutes, or until evenly
browned.

### COOK'S TIP

When preparing lemongrass,
take care to remove the outer
layers, which can be tough and
fibrous. Use only the tender part
at the center, which has the
finest flavor.

3 Add the bell pepper and stir-fry for
an additional 3–4 minutes. Add
the chili and bean sprouts and stir-fry
for 2 minutes. Mix the lemongrass,
peanut butter, coconut milk, rice
vinegar, soy sauce, and sugar together
in a bowl, then stir into the skillet.

4 Meanwhile, cook the egg noodles
in boiling salted water for
4 minutes, or according to the package
directions. Drain and stir into the
skillet, tossing to mix evenly.

5 Season to taste with salt and
pepper. Sprinkle with the reserved
scallions and serve hot.

# red-hot beef with cashew nuts

## serves four

1 lb 2 oz/500 g lean boneless
  beef sirloin
1 tsp vegetable oil
MARINADE
1 tbsp sesame seeds
1 garlic clove, chopped
1 tbsp finely chopped fresh
  gingerroot
1 fresh red Thai chili, chopped
2 tbsp dark soy sauce
1 tsp Thai red curry paste
TO FINISH
1 tsp sesame oil
4 tbsp unsalted cashew nuts
1 scallion, thickly
  sliced diagonally
cucumber slices, to garnish

1 Using a sharp knife, cut the beef into ½-inch/1-cm wide strips. Place them in a large, nonmetallic bowl.

2 To make the marinade, toast the sesame seeds in a heavy-bottom skillet over medium heat for 2–3 minutes, or until golden brown, shaking the skillet occasionally.

3 Place the seeds in a mortar with the garlic, ginger, and chili and, using a pestle, grind to a smooth paste. Add the soy sauce and curry paste and mix well.

4 Spoon the paste over the beef strips and toss to coat the meat evenly. Cover and let marinate in the refrigerator for at least 2–3 hours or overnight.

5 Heat a heavy-bottom skillet or ridged grill pan until very hot and brush with vegetable oil. Place the beef strips in the skillet and cook quickly, turning frequently, until lightly browned. Remove the skillet from the heat and spoon the beef into a pile on a hot serving dish.

6 Heat the sesame oil in a small skillet. Add the cashew nuts and quickly cook until golden. Add the scallion and stir-fry for 30 seconds. Sprinkle the mixture on top of the beef strips, then garnish with cucumber slices and serve immediately.

# beef satay with peanut sauce

## serves four

1 lb 2 oz/500 g lean beef fillet

2 garlic cloves, crushed

¾-inch/2-cm piece fresh gingerroot, finely grated

1 tbsp brown sugar

1 tbsp dark soy sauce

1 tbsp lime juice

2 tsp sesame oil

1 tsp ground coriander

1 tsp ground turmeric

½ tsp chili powder

PEANUT SAUCE

1¼ cups coconut milk

8 tbsp chunky peanut butter

½ small onion, grated

2 tsp brown sugar

½ tsp chili powder

1 tbsp dark soy sauce

TO GARNISH

chopped cucumber

red bell pepper pieces

1 Cut the beef into ½-inch/1-cm cubes and place in a large bowl.

2 Add the garlic, ginger, sugar, soy sauce, lime juice, sesame oil, coriander, turmeric, and chili powder. Mix well to coat the pieces of meat evenly. Cover and let marinate in the refrigerator for at least 2 hours or overnight.

3 Preheat the broiler to high. To make the peanut sauce, place all the ingredients in a small pan and stir over medium heat until boiling. Remove the pan from the heat and keep warm.

4 Thread the beef cubes on to presoaked bamboo skewers. Cook the skewers under the hot broiler for 3–5 minutes, turning frequently, until golden. Alternatively, grill over hot coals. Transfer to a large serving plate, then garnish with chopped cucumber and red bell pepper pieces and serve with the peanut sauce.

# hot beef & coconut curry

## serves four

1¾ cups coconut milk

2 tbsp Thai red curry paste

2 garlic cloves, crushed

1 lb 2 oz/500 g braising steak

2 fresh kaffir lime leaves, shredded

3 tbsp lime juice

2 tbsp Thai fish sauce

1 large fresh red chili, seeded
    and sliced

½ tsp ground turmeric

salt and pepper

2 tbsp chopped fresh basil leaves

2 tbsp chopped cilantro leaves

shredded coconut, to garnish

freshly cooked rice, to serve

1 Place the coconut milk in a large pan and bring to a boil. Reduce the heat and simmer gently for 10 minutes, or until it has thickened. Stir in the curry paste and garlic and simmer for an additional 5 minutes.

2 Cut the beef into ¾-inch/ 2-cm chunks. Add to the pan and bring to a boil, stirring constantly. Reduce the heat and add the kaffir lime leaves, lime juice, fish sauce, sliced chili, turmeric, and ½ teaspoon of salt.

3 Cover the pan and continue simmering for 20–25 minutes, or until the meat is tender, adding a little water if the sauce looks too dry.

4 Stir in the basil and cilantro and season to taste with salt and pepper. Sprinkle with shredded coconut and serve with freshly cooked rice.

# spicy fried ground pork

## serves four

2 garlic cloves

3 shallots

1-inch/2.5-cm piece fresh
    gingerroot

2 tbsp corn oil

1 lb 2 oz/500 g ground lean pork

2 tbsp Thai fish sauce

1 tbsp dark soy sauce

1 tbsp Thai red curry paste

4 dried kaffir lime leaves, crumbled

4 plum tomatoes, chopped

3 tbsp chopped cilantro

salt and pepper

TO GARNISH

cilantro sprigs

scallion tassels (see Cook's Tip)

freshly cooked fine egg noodles,
    to serve

1 Finely chop the garlic, shallots, and ginger. Heat the oil in a large skillet or preheated wok over medium heat. Add the garlic, shallots, and ginger and stir-fry for 2 minutes. Stir in the pork and continue stir-frying until golden brown.

2 Stir in the fish sauce, soy sauce, curry paste, and lime leaves and stir-fry for an additional 1–2 minutes over high heat.

3 Add the chopped tomatoes and cook for an additional 5–6 minutes, stirring occasionally. Stir in the chopped cilantro and season to taste with salt and pepper.

4 Serve hot, spooned onto freshly cooked fine egg noodles, garnished with cilantro sprigs and scallion tassels.

### COOK'S TIP

To make the scallion tassels, make a few cuts lengthwise down the stem of each scallion. Place in a bowl of ice-cold water and let stand until the tassels open out. Drain well before using.

# roasted red pork

## serves four

1 lb 5 oz/600 g pork fillets

Napa cabbage, shredded

1 fresh red chili flower (see page
160), to garnish

MARINADE

2 garlic cloves, crushed

1 tbsp grated fresh gingerroot

1 tbsp light soy sauce

1 tbsp Thai fish sauce

1 tbsp rice wine or dry sherry

1 tbsp hoisin sauce

1 tbsp sesame oil

1 tbsp palm sugar or
brown sugar

½ tsp Chinese five-spice powder

few drops of red food coloring
(optional)

1 Mix all the ingredients for the marinade together in a small bowl, then spread over the pork, turning to coat evenly. Place in a large, nonmetallic dish, then cover and let marinate in the refrigerator overnight.

2 Preheat the oven to 425°F/220°C. Place a rack in a roasting pan, then half fill the pan with boiling water. Lift the pork from the marinade and place on the rack. Reserve the marinade.

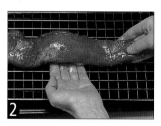

**VARIATION**

The pork may also be broiled. Cut the meat into slices or strips and coat in the marinade, then arrange on a foil-lined broiler pan and broil under high heat, turning occasionally and basting with the marinade.

3 Roast in the preheated oven for 20 minutes. Baste with the marinade, then reduce the heat to 350°F/180°C and continue roasting for an additional 35–40 minutes, basting occasionally with the marinade, until the pork is a rich, reddish brown and thoroughly cooked.

4 Cut the pork into slices and arrange on a bed of shredded Napa cabbage. Garnish with a red chili flower and serve.

# pork steaks with lemongrass

## serves four

2 lemongrass stems, outer
  leaves removed
2 garlic cloves, crushed
½ tsp pepper
1 tbsp sugar
2 tbsp Thai fish sauce
2 tbsp soy sauce
1 tbsp sesame oil
1 tbsp lime juice
4 scallions, finely chopped
2 tbsp coconut milk
4 pork steaks
lime wedges, to garnish

---

### VARIATION
The pork steaks are perfect for
cooking over medium–hot coals
on the grill.

---

1 Finely chop the lemongrass and
place in a bowl with the garlic,
pepper, sugar, fish sauce, soy sauce,
oil, lime juice, scallions, and coconut
milk. Mix well to combine.

2 Place the pork steaks in a large,
shallow, nonmetallic dish. Pour
over the marinade and turn the steaks
until coated. Cover the dish with plastic
wrap and let marinate in the
refrigerator for 1 hour.

3 Preheat the broiler to medium.
Cook the pork steaks under the
hot broiler for 5 minutes on each side,
or until cooked through. Garnish with
lime wedges and serve immediately.

# stir-fried pork & corn

## serves four

2 tbsp vegetable oil

1 lb 2 oz/500 g lean boneless pork,
 cut into thin strips

1 garlic clove, chopped

3 cups fresh corn kernels

1⅓ cups green beans, cut into
 short lengths

2 scallions, chopped

1 small fresh red chili, chopped

1 tsp sugar

1 tbsp light soy sauce

3 tbsp chopped cilantro

freshly cooked egg noodles or rice,
 to serve

### COOK'S TIP

In Thailand, long beans would be used for dishes such as this, but you can substitute green beans, which are more easily available. Look out for long beans in Asian food stores—they are like long string beans and have a similar flavor, but their texture is crisp, and they cook more quickly.

1 Heat the oil in a large skillet or preheated wok. Add the pork and stir-fry quickly over high heat until lightly browned.

2 Stir in the garlic, corn, beans, scallions, and chili and continue stir-frying over high heat for 2–3 minutes, or until the vegetables are heated through and almost tender.

3 Stir in the sugar and soy sauce and stir-fry for an additional 30 seconds over high heat.

4 Sprinkle with the cilantro and serve immediately with freshly cooked egg noodles or rice.

# pork with soy & sesame glaze

## serves four

2 pork fillets, about
    9½ oz/275 g each
2 tbsp dark soy sauce
2 tbsp clear honey
2 garlic cloves, crushed
1 tbsp sesame seeds
1 onion, thinly sliced into rings
1 tbsp all-purpose flour, seasoned
corn oil, for frying
crisp salad greens, to serve

1 Preheat the oven to 400°F/200°C. Trim the pork fillets and place in a wide, nonmetallic dish.

2 Mix the soy sauce, honey, and garlic together in a small bowl, then spread over the pork, turning to coat evenly.

3 Lift the pork fillets into a roasting pan or shallow, ovenproof dish and sprinkle evenly with sesame seeds.

4 Roast the pork in the preheated oven for 20 minutes, spooning over any juices. Cover loosely with foil to prevent overbrowning and roast for an additional 10–15 minutes, or until the meat is thoroughly cooked.

5 Meanwhile, dip the onion slices in the seasoned flour and shake off the excess. Heat the oil in a small skillet. Add the onion rings and cook until golden and crisp, turning occasionally. Serve the pork in slices with the fried onions on a bed of crisp salad greens.

# tamarind pork

## serves four

2 tbsp vegetable oil

1 lb 5 oz/600 g lean boneless pork,
    cut into thin strips

generous 2¼ cups canned bamboo
    shoots, drained

freshly cooked noodles, to serve

SPICE PASTE

1-inch/2.5-cm piece fresh
    gingerroot

4 shallots, finely chopped

2 garlic cloves, finely chopped

1 tsp ground coriander

2 fresh red chilies, seeded and
    finely chopped

½ tsp ground turmeric

6 blanched almonds, finely chopped

2 tbsp tamarind paste

2 tbsp hot water

1 To make the spice paste, peel the
    ginger and finely chop. Place the
shallots, garlic, ginger, coriander,
chilies, turmeric, almonds, tamarind
paste, and water in a food processor
and process until smooth.

2 Heat the oil in a preheated wok
    or skillet over high heat. Add the
pork and cook for 3 minutes, or until
the meat is colored. Add the spice
paste and continue to cook for an
additional 2–3 minutes.

3 Add the bamboo shoots and cook
    for an additional 2 minutes, or
until the pork is cooked through. Serve
with freshly cooked noodles.

**VARIATION**

If you cannot find shallots,

replace them with

ordinary small onions.

# spiced pork sausages

## serves four

3½ cups ground lean pork

scant ¾ cup cooked rice

1 garlic clove, crushed

1 tsp Thai red curry paste

1 tsp pepper

1 tsp ground coriander

½ tsp salt

3 tbsp lime juice

2 tbsp chopped cilantro

3 tbsp peanut oil

TO GARNISH

cucumber slices

fresh red chili strips

Chili & Coconut Sambal (see page
    176) or soy sauce, to serve

3 Heat the oil in a large skillet over medium heat. Add the sausages, in batches if necessary, and cook for 8–10 minutes, turning them over occasionally, until they are evenly golden brown and cooked through. Transfer to a serving plate, then garnish with cucumber slices and a few strips of red chili and serve hot with Chili & Coconut Sambal or soy sauce.

**COOK'S TIP**

These sausages can also be served as an appetizer—shape the mixture slightly smaller to make 16 bite-size sausages. Serve with a soy dipping sauce.

1 Place the pork, rice, garlic, curry paste, pepper, coriander, salt, lime juice, and chopped cilantro in a bowl and knead together with your hands to mix evenly.

2 Use your hands to form the mixture into 12 small sausage shapes. Using sausage casings, if available, will help to keep the sausages together when cooked.

# thai-style burgers

## serves four

1 small lemongrass stem

1 small fresh red chili, seeded

2 garlic cloves

2 scallions

7 oz/200 g closed-cup mushrooms

3½ cups ground lean pork

1 tbsp Thai fish sauce

3 tbsp chopped cilantro

salt and pepper

all-purpose flour, for dusting

corn oil, for pan-frying

2 tbsp mayonnaise

1 tbsp lime juice

TO SERVE

4 sesame hamburger buns

shredded Napa cabbage

1 Place the lemongrass, chili, garlic, and scallions in a food processor and process to a smooth paste. Add the mushrooms and process until very finely chopped.

2 Add the pork, fish sauce, and cilantro. Season well with salt and pepper, then divide the mixture into 4 equal portions and form into flat burger shapes with lightly floured hands.

**COOK'S TIP**

You can add a spoonful of your favorite relish to each burger, or add a few Crisp Pickled Vegetables (see page 166) for a change of texture.

3 Heat the oil in a skillet over medium heat. Add the burgers and cook for 6–8 minutes, until cooked.

4 Meanwhile, mix the mayonnaise with the lime juice in a small bowl. Split the hamburger buns and spread the lime-flavored mayonnaise on the cut surfaces. Add shredded Napa cabbage, then top with a burger and sandwich together. Serve.

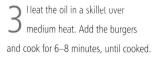

# lamb with lime leaves

## serves four

2 fresh red Thai chilies

2 tbsp peanut oil

2 garlic cloves, crushed

4 shallots, chopped

2 lemongrass stems, sliced

6 fresh kaffir lime leaves

1 tbsp tamarind paste

2 tbsp palm sugar

1 lb/450 g lean boneless lamb

    (leg or loin fillet)

2½ cups coconut milk

6 oz/175 g cherry tomatoes, halved

1 tbsp chopped cilantro

freshly cooked Thai fragrant rice,

    to serve

1 Using a sharp knife, seed and very finely chop the chilies. Reserve until required.

2 Heat the oil in a large, preheated wok. Add the garlic, shallots, lemongrass, lime leaves, tamarind paste, sugar, and chilies to the wok and stir-fry for 2 minutes.

3 Using a sharp knife, cut the lamb into thin strips or cubes.

4 Add the lamb to the wok and stir-fry for 5 minutes, tossing well so that the lamb is evenly coated in the spice mixture.

5 Pour the coconut milk into the wok and bring to a boil. Reduce the heat and let simmer for 20 minutes.

6 Add the cherry tomatoes and chopped cilantro to the wok and simmer for 5 minutes. Transfer to serving plates and serve hot with fragrant rice.

### COOK'S TIP

Peanut oil is used here for flavor—it is a common oil used for stir-frying.

# red lamb curry

## serves four

1 lb 2 oz/500 g lean boneless
　leg of lamb
2 tbsp vegetable oil
1 large onion, sliced
2 garlic cloves, crushed
2 tbsp Thai red curry paste
⅔ cup coconut milk
1 tbsp brown sugar
1 large red bell pepper, seeded and
　thickly sliced
½ cup lamb or beef stock
1 tbsp Thai fish sauce
2 tbsp lime juice
generous 1 cup canned
　water chestnuts, drained
2 tbsp chopped cilantro
2 tbsp chopped fresh basil
salt and pepper
fresh basil leaves, to garnish
freshly cooked jasmine rice, to serve

**VARIATION**

This curry can also be made with other lean red meats. Try replacing the lamb with trimmed duck breasts or pieces of lean braising beef. This richly spiced curry uses the typically red-hot chili flavor of Thai red curry paste, made with dried red chilies, to give it a warm, russet-red color.

1 Trim the meat and cut it into 1¼-inch/3-cm cubes. Heat the oil in a large skillet or preheated wok over high heat. Add the onion and garlic and stir-fry for 2–3 minutes to soften. Add the meat and stir-fry the mixture quickly until lightly browned.

2 Stir in the curry paste and cook for a few seconds, then add the coconut milk and sugar and bring to a boil. Reduce the heat and simmer for 15 minutes, stirring occasionally.

3 Stir in the bell pepper, stock, fish sauce, and lime juice, then cover and simmer for an additional 15 minutes, or until the meat is tender.

4 Add the water chestnuts, cilantro, and basil and season to taste with salt and pepper. Transfer to serving plates, then garnish with basil leaves and serve with jasmine rice.

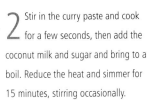

# stir-fried lamb with mint

generous ⅓ cup fresh mint leaves

2 tbsp vegetable oil

2 garlic cloves, finely sliced

2 fresh red chilies, seeded and
   cut into thin strips

1 onion, thinly sliced

1½ tbsp Madras curry paste

1 lb 2 oz/500 g lamb fillet, cut
   into thin strips

8 oz/225 g canned baby
   corn cobs, drained

4 scallions, finely chopped

1 tbsp Thai fish sauce

freshly cooked rice, to serve

---

**VARIATION**

You can use fresh baby corn
cobs, halved, instead of
canned ones, if you prefer.

---

1 Coarsely shred the mint leaves
and reserve until required. Heat
half the oil in a preheated wok or large
skillet. Add the garlic and chilies and
cook until soft. Remove and reserve.
Add the onion and cook for 5 minutes,
or until soft. Remove and reserve.

2 Heat the remaining oil in the wok.
Add the curry paste and cook for
1 minute. Add the lamb, in batches if
necessary, and cook for 5–8 minutes,
or until cooked through and tender.

3 Return the onion to the wok with
the baby corn cobs, scallions,
mint, and fish sauce. Cook until heated
through. Sprinkle the garlic and chilies
over and serve with rice.

# roast chicken with ginger & lime

## serves four

1¼-inch/3-cm piece fresh
    gingerroot, finely chopped

2 garlic cloves, finely chopped

1 small onion, finely chopped

1 lemongrass stem, finely chopped

½ tsp salt

1 tsp black peppercorns

3 lb 5 oz/1.5 kg roasting chicken

1 tbsp coconut cream

2 tbsp lime juice

2 tbsp clear honey

1 tsp cornstarch

2 tsp water

stir-fried vegetables, to serve

1 Place the ginger, garlic, onion, lemongrass, salt, and peppercorns in a mortar and, using a pestle, grind to a smooth paste.

2 Using poultry shears or strong kitchen scissors, cut the chicken in half lengthwise. Spread the paste all over the chicken, both inside and out, and spread it on to the flesh under the breast skin. Cover and let chill in the refrigerator for at least several hours or overnight.

3 Preheat the oven to 350°F/180°C. Heat the coconut cream, lime juice, and honey together in a small pan, stirring until smooth. Brush a little of the mixture evenly over the chicken.

4 Place the chicken halves on a baking sheet over a roasting pan half filled with boiling water. Roast in the preheated oven for 1 hour, or until the chicken is a rich golden brown color, basting occasionally with the lime and honey mixture.

5 When the chicken is cooked, boil the water from the roasting pan to reduce it to a scant ½ cup. Blend the cornstarch and water together and stir into the reduced liquid. Bring gently to a boil, then stir until slightly thickened and clear. Serve the chicken with the sauce and freshly cooked stir-fried vegetables.

# red chicken with cherry tomatoes

## serves four

1 tbsp corn oil

1 lb/450 g skinless,
  boneless chicken

2 garlic cloves, crushed

2 tbsp Thai red curry paste

2 tbsp grated fresh galangal or
  gingerroot

1 tbsp tamarind paste

4 fresh kaffir lime leaves

8 oz/225 g sweet potato

2½ cups coconut milk

8 oz/225 g cherry tomatoes, halved

3 tbsp chopped cilantro

freshly cooked jasmine or Thai
  fragrant rice, to serve

1 Heat the oil in a large,
  preheated wok.

2 Using a sharp knife, thinly slice
  the chicken. Add the chicken to
the wok and stir-fry for 5 minutes.

3 Add the garlic, curry paste,
  galangal, tamarind paste, and
lime leaves to the wok and stir-fry for
1 minute.

4 Using a sharp knife, peel and dice
  the sweet potato.

5 Add the coconut milk and sweet
  potato to the mixture in the wok
and bring to a boil. Let bubble over
medium heat for 20 minutes, or until
the juices begin to thicken and reduce.

6 Add the cherry tomatoes and
  cilantro to the curry and cook for
an additional 5 minutes, stirring
occasionally. Transfer to serving plates
and serve hot with jasmine or Thai
fragrant rice.

# green chicken curry

6 skinless, boneless chicken thighs

1¾ cups coconut milk

2 garlic cloves, crushed

2 tbsp Thai fish sauce

2 tbsp Thai green curry paste

12 baby eggplants

3 fresh green chilies, finely chopped

3 fresh kaffir lime leaves, shredded,
    plus extra to garnish (optional)

salt and pepper

4 tbsp chopped cilantro

freshly cooked rice, to serve

1 Cut the chicken into bite-size pieces. Pour the coconut milk into a preheated wok or large skillet over high heat and bring to a boil.

2 Add the chicken, garlic, and fish sauce to the wok and return to a boil. Reduce the heat and simmer gently for 30 minutes, or until the chicken is just tender.

3 Remove the chicken from the wok with a slotted spoon. Keep warm.

4 Stir the curry paste into the wok. Add the eggplants, chilies, and lime leaves and simmer for 5 minutes.

5 Return the chicken to the wok and bring to a boil. Season to taste with salt and pepper, then stir in the cilantro. Transfer to serving plates and garnish with lime leaves, if using. Serve immediately with freshly cooked rice.

### COOK'S TIP

Baby eggplants, or "Asian eggplants" as they are also known, are traditionally used in this curry, but they are not always available. If you can't find them in an Asian food store, use chopped ordinary eggplant, or substitute a few green peas.

# chicken & mango stir-fry

## serves four

6 skinless, boneless chicken thighs

1-inch/2.5-cm piece fresh
gingerroot, grated

1 garlic clove, crushed

1 small fresh red chili, seeded
and chopped

1 large red bell pepper, seeded

4 scallions

2 cups snow peas

3½ oz/100 g baby corn cobs

1 large firm ripe mango

2 tbsp corn oil

1 tbsp light soy sauce

3 tbsp rice wine or dry sherry

1 tsp sesame oil

salt and pepper

snipped fresh chives, to garnish

1 Cut the chicken into long, thin strips and place in a bowl. Mix the ginger, garlic, and chili together in a separate bowl, then stir into the chicken strips to coat them evenly.

2 Slice the bell pepper thinly, cutting diagonally. Diagonally slice the scallions. Cut the snow peas and baby corn cobs in half diagonally. Peel the mango, then remove the pit and slice the flesh thinly.

3 Heat the corn oil in a large skillet or preheated wok over high heat.

4 Add the chicken and stir-fry for 4–5 minutes, until just turning golden brown. Add the bell pepper and stir-fry over medium heat for 4–5 minutes, or until soft.

5 Add the scallions, snow peas, and baby corn cobs and stir-fry for an additional 1 minute.

6 Mix the soy sauce, rice wine, and sesame oil together in a small bowl and stir it into the skillet. Add the mango and stir gently for 1 minute to heat thoroughly. Season to taste with salt and pepper and serve immediately, garnished with snipped chives.

# stir-fried chicken with thai basil

## serves four

1 lb 5 oz/600 g skinless, boneless
   chicken breast fillets
2 tbsp vegetable oil
4 garlic cloves, crushed
4 scallions, finely chopped
4 fresh green chilies, seeded and
   finely chopped
1 green bell pepper, seeded and
   thinly sliced
generous ½ cup fresh Thai basil
   leaves, coarsely chopped
2 tbsp Thai fish sauce
fresh basil leaves, to garnish
freshly cooked rice, to serve

1 Using a sharp knife, cut the chicken into thin strips.

2 Heat the oil in a preheated wok. Add the garlic and scallions and cook for 2 minutes. Add the chilies and bell pepper and cook for an additional 2 minutes.

3 Add the chicken and cook until browned. Stir in the basil and fish sauce and stir-fry until the chicken is cooked through. Garnish with basil leaves and serve with rice.

### COOK'S TIP
Thai basil is available in Asian
food stores. If you cannot find it,
omit it from the recipe.

# chicken with lemongrass & chili

## serves four

2 fresh red chilies

2 tbsp vegetable oil

4 garlic cloves, thinly sliced

1 onion, thinly sliced

2 lemongrass stems, outer part
    removed, very finely chopped

8 chicken thighs with bones
    and skin

3 tbsp Thai fish sauce

1 tbsp brown sugar

1 cup chicken stock

### COOK'S TIP

If the chicken mixture becomes
too dry during cooking, add a
little water.

1 Using a small knife, seed and finely chop the chilies. Heat the oil in a large skillet. Add the garlic and onion and cook gently for 5–10 minutes, or until soft.

2 Add the lemongrass and chilies and cook for 2 minutes. Add the chicken and cook for 5 minutes, or until browned all over.

3 Add the fish sauce, sugar, and stock. Bring to a boil, then reduce the heat and simmer, covered, for 30 minutes, or until the chicken is cooked through. Serve immediately.

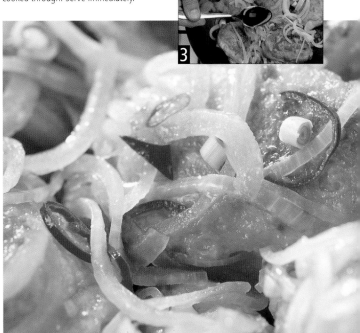

# spiced cilantro chicken

## serves four

4 skinless, boneless chicken breasts

2 garlic cloves

1 fresh green chili, seeded

¾-inch/2-cm piece fresh gingerroot

4 tbsp chopped cilantro

finely grated rind of 1 lime

3 tbsp lime juice

2 tbsp light soy sauce

1 tbsp superfine sugar

¾ cup coconut milk

TO GARNISH

finely chopped cilantro

cucumber slices

radish slices

½ fresh red chili, seeded and sliced
   into rings

freshly cooked rice, to serve

1 Using a sharp knife, cut 3 deep slashes into the skinned side of each chicken breast. Place the breasts in a single layer in a nonmetallic dish.

2 Place the garlic, chili, ginger, cilantro, lime rind and juice, soy sauce, sugar, and coconut milk in a food processor and process to a smooth paste.

3 Spread the paste over both sides of the chicken breasts, coating them evenly. Cover with plastic wrap and let marinate in the refrigerator for 1 hour.

4 Preheat the broiler to medium. Lift the chicken from the marinade, then drain off the excess and place on a broiler pan. Cook under the hot broiler for 12–15 minutes, or until thoroughly and evenly cooked.

5 Meanwhile, place the remaining marinade in a pan and bring to a boil. Reduce the heat and simmer for several minutes. Transfer the chicken breasts to serving plates. Garnish with chopped cilantro, cucumber slices, radish slices, and chili rings and serve with rice.

# quick green chicken curry

6 scallions

1 tbsp vegetable oil

1 lb 5oz/600 g skinless, boneless
    chicken breast, cut into cubes

generous ¾ cup coconut cream

3 tbsp Thai green curry paste

3 tbsp chopped cilantro

freshly cooked noodles, to serve

---

### COOK'S TIP

Store scallions in the salad
compartment of the refrigerator.
They will keep for up to 3 days.

---

1 Using a small knife, slice the
scallions. Heat the oil in a large
skillet. Add the scallions and the
chicken and cook, stirring constantly,
for 3–4 minutes, or until the chicken
is browned.

2 Stir in the coconut cream and
curry paste and cook for an
additional 5 minutes, or until the
chicken is cooked through. Add a little
water or stock if the sauce becomes
too thick.

3 Stir in the chopped cilantro
and serve immediately with
freshly cooked noodles.

# braised chicken with garlic & spices

4 garlic cloves, chopped

4 shallots, chopped

2 small fresh red chilies, seeded and
   chopped

1 lemongrass stem, finely chopped

1 tbsp chopped cilantro

1 tsp shrimp paste

½ tsp ground cinnamon

1 tbsp tamarind paste

2 tbsp vegetable oil

8 small chicken joints, such as
   drumsticks or thighs

1¼ cups chicken stock

1 tbsp Thai fish sauce

1 tbsp smooth peanut butter

salt and pepper

4 tbsp toasted peanuts, chopped

TO SERVE

stir-fried vegetables

freshly cooked noodles

1 Place the garlic, shallots, chilies, lemongrass, cilantro, and shrimp paste in a mortar and, using a pestle, grind to an almost smooth paste. Add the cinnamon and tamarind paste to the mixture.

2 Heat the oil in a wide skillet or preheated wok. Add the chicken joints, turning frequently, until golden brown on all sides. Remove the chicken from the skillet and keep hot. Tip away any excess fat.

3 Add the spice paste to the skillet and stir over medium heat until lightly browned. Stir in the stock, then return the chicken joints to the skillet.

4 Bring to a boil, then cover tightly and reduce the heat. Let simmer for 25–30 minutes, stirring occasionally, until the chicken is tender and thoroughly cooked. Stir in the fish sauce and peanut butter and simmer for an additional 10 minutes.

5 Season to taste with salt and pepper and sprinkle the toasted peanuts over the chicken. Serve hot with stir-fried vegetables and noodles.

# peanut-crusted chicken

## serves six

2 garlic cloves, crushed

1-inch/2.5-cm piece fresh
   gingerroot, finely grated

1 lemongrass stem, outer leaves
   removed, finely chopped

2 tbsp chopped cilantro leaves

scant 1¼ cups salted peanuts

¾ cup all-purpose flour

2 eggs

4 tbsp milk

12 chicken drumsticks, skin removed

vegetable oil, for oiling

DIPPING SAUCE

1 fresh red chili, seeded and
   finely chopped

2 garlic cloves, crushed

½ cup white wine vinegar

2 tbsp brown sugar

1 Preheat the oven to 425°F/220°C. Place the garlic, ginger, lemongrass, cilantro leaves, peanuts, and 2 tablespoons of the flour in a food processor and process until finely ground. Transfer to a shallow dish.

2 Beat the eggs and milk together in a bowl. Spread the remaining flour on a plate. Dip the drumsticks into the flour, then into the egg mixture, and finally into the peanut mixture. Arrange them in an oiled roasting pan.

3 Bake in the preheated oven for 15 minutes, then turn them and cook for an additional 15 minutes. Pour off any excess oil and cook the drumsticks for 5 minutes, or until crisp.

4 To make the sauce, place the chili and garlic in a mortar and, using a pestle, grind to a paste. Place the vinegar and sugar in a pan and heat gently until the sugar dissolves. Bring to a boil and simmer for 2 minutes. Stir in the chili-garlic paste. Transfer to a bowl. Drain the drumsticks on paper towels and serve with the sauce.

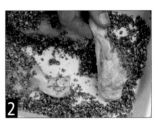

# duck breasts with chili & lime

## serves four

4 boneless duck breasts

2 garlic cloves, crushed

4 tsp brown sugar

3 tbsp lime juice

1 tbsp soy sauce

1 tsp chili sauce

1 tsp vegetable oil

2 tbsp plum jelly

½ cup chicken stock

salt and pepper

TO SERVE

freshly cooked rice

crisp salad greens

1 Using a small, sharp knife, cut deep slashes in the skin of the duck to make a diamond pattern. Place the duck breasts in a wide, nonmetallic dish.

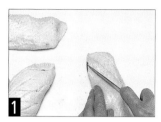

2 Mix the garlic, sugar, lime juice, soy sauce, and chili sauce together in a bowl, then spoon over the duck breasts, turning well to coat evenly. Cover and let marinate in the refrigerator for at least 3 hours or overnight.

3 Drain the duck, reserving the marinade. Heat a large, heavy-bottom skillet until very hot and brush with the oil. Add the duck breasts, skin-side down, and cook for 5 minutes, or until the skin is browned and crisp. Tip away the excess fat. Turn the duck breasts over.

4 Continue cooking on the other side for 2–3 minutes to brown. Add the reserved marinade, plum jelly, and stock and simmer for 2 minutes. Season to taste with salt and pepper. Transfer to individual serving plates, then spoon over the pan juices and serve hot with freshly cooked rice and crisp salad greens.

# roasted duckling with pineapple & coconut

## serves four

3 lb 8 oz/1.6 kg duckling

salt and pepper

2 tbsp peanut oil

1 small pineapple

1 large onion, chopped

1 garlic clove, finely chopped

1 tsp finely chopped fresh
  gingerroot

½ tsp ground coriander

1 tbsp Thai green curry paste

1 tsp brown sugar

1¾ cup coconut milk

cilantro, chopped

fresh red and green chili flowers,
  to garnish (see page 160)

freshly cooked jasmine rice, to serve

1 Preheat the broiler to medium. Using a large knife or poultry shears, cut the duckling in half lengthwise, cutting through the line of the breastbone. Wipe inside and out with paper towels. Sprinkle with salt and pepper to taste, then prick the skin with a fork and brush with oil.

2 Place the duckling, cut-side down, on a broiler pan and cook under the broiler for 25–30 minutes, turning occasionally, until golden brown. Tip away any fat that builds up in the broiler pan, as it may burn.

3 Let the duck cool, then cut each half into 2 portions. Peel and core the pineapple, then cut the flesh into dice shapes. Reserve.

4 Heat the remaining oil in a large skillet. Add the onion and garlic and cook for 3–4 minutes, or until softened. Stir in the ginger, coriander, curry paste, and sugar and stir-fry for 1 minute.

5 Stir in the coconut milk and bring to a boil. Add the duckling portions and the pineapple. Reduce the heat and simmer for 5 minutes. Sprinkle with cilantro and garnish with red and green chili flowers. Serve over freshly cooked jasmine rice.

# Rice & Noodles

With its monsoon climate and abundant rainfall, Thailand has the ideal conditions for rice growing and has become one of the major rice producers in the world. It is thought that rice grew there as far back as 3500 B.C., so it's not surprising that rice is the staple food of Thailand.

Two main varieties of rice are used in Thai cooking—long-grain and short-grain. The long-grain is Thai fragrant rice, a good quality, white, fluffy rice with delicately scented, separate grains. Glutinous or "sticky" rice is a short-grain rice with a high starch content that causes the grains to stick together.

Noodles also play a vital part in Thai meals, and street vendors serve them as a snack at all times of the day. Rice noodles in flat ribbons (sticks) or thin vermicelli are the most common. Cellophane (mung bean) noodles are also locally made, but egg noodles are often imported from China.

# crispy rice noodles

## serves four

vegetable oil, for deep-frying,
   plus 1½ tbsp

7 oz/200 g rice vermicelli noodles

1 onion, finely chopped

4 garlic cloves, finely chopped

1 skinless, boneless chicken breast,
   finely chopped

2 fresh red Thai chilies,
   seeded and sliced

4 tbsp dried shiitake mushrooms,
   soaked and thinly sliced

3 tbsp dried shrimp

4 scallions, sliced

3 tbsp lime juice

2 tbsp soy sauce

2 tbsp Thai fish sauce

2 tbsp rice vinegar or white
   wine vinegar

2 tbsp brown sugar

2 eggs, beaten

3 tbsp chopped cilantro

scallion curls, to garnish
   (see page 212)

1 Heat the oil for deep-frying in a large skillet or preheated wok until very hot. Add the rice noodles and deep-fry quickly, occasionally turning them, until puffed up, crisp, and pale golden brown. Lift on to paper towels and drain well.

2 Heat 1 tablespoon of the remaining oil in a separate skillet. Add the onion and garlic and cook for 1 minute. Add the chicken and stir-fry for 3 minutes. Finally, add the chilies, mushrooms, dried shrimp, and scallions.

3 Mix the lime juice, soy sauce, fish sauce, rice vinegar, and sugar together in a bowl, then stir into the skillet and cook for an additional 1 minute. Remove the skillet from the heat.

4 Heat the remaining oil in a wide skillet. Pour in the eggs to coat the bottom of the skillet evenly, making a thin omelet. Cook until set and golden, then turn it over and cook the other side. Turn out and roll up, then slice into long ribbon strips.

5 Toss the fried noodles, stir-fried ingredients, cilantro, and omelet strips together. Garnish with scallion curls and serve.

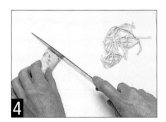

# rice noodles with mushrooms & tofu

## serves four

8 oz/225 g rice stick noodles

2 tbsp vegetable oil

1 garlic clove, finely chopped

¾-inch/2-cm piece fresh gingerroot, finely chopped

4 shallots, thinly sliced

1¼ cups sliced shiitake mushrooms

3½ oz/100 g firm tofu (drained weight), cut into ⅝-inch/ 1.5-cm dice shapes

2 tbsp light soy sauce

1 tbsp rice wine or dry sherry

1 tbsp Thai fish sauce

1 tbsp smooth peanut butter

1 tsp chili sauce

2 tbsp toasted peanuts, chopped

shredded fresh basil leaves

**1** Place the rice noodles in a bowl, then cover with hot water and let soak for 15 minutes, or according to the package directions. Drain well.

**2** Heat the oil in a large skillet. Add the garlic, ginger, and shallots and stir-fry for 1–2 minutes, or until softened and lightly browned.

**3** Add the mushrooms and stir-fry for an additional 2–3 minutes. Stir in the tofu and toss gently to brown lightly.

**4** Mix the soy sauce, rice wine, fish sauce, peanut butter, and chili sauce together in a small bowl, then stir into the skillet.

**5** Stir in the rice noodles and toss to coat evenly in the sauce. Sprinkle with peanuts and shredded basil leaves and serve hot.

### VARIATION

For an easy pantry dish, replace the shiitake mushrooms with canned Chinese straw mushrooms. Alternatively, use dried shiitake mushrooms, soaked and drained before use.

# noodles with shrimp & green bell peppers

## serves four

9 oz/250 g rice noodles

1 tbsp vegetable oil

2 garlic cloves, crushed

1 fresh red chili, seeded and
   thinly sliced

1 green bell pepper, seeded and
   thinly sliced

6 scallions, coarsely chopped

2 tsp cornstarch

2 tbsp oyster sauce

1 tbsp Thai fish sauce

1 tsp sugar

1 cup chicken stock

9 oz/250 g small cooked
   shrimp, shelled

**2** Heat the oil in a preheated wok. Add the garlic, chili, bell pepper, and scallions. Cook for 1 minute, then transfer to a plate and reserve.

**3** Blend the cornstarch with a little water and add to the wok with the oyster sauce, fish sauce, sugar, and stock. Stir over medium heat until the mixture boils and thickens.

**4** Return the bell pepper and scallion mixture to the wok with the shrimp and noodles. Cook, stirring, for 2 minutes, or until heated through. Transfer to a heated serving bowl and serve immediately.

**1** Prepare the noodles according to the package directions. Drain, then rinse under cold water and drain again.

# sesame noodles with shrimp & cilantro

## serves four

1 garlic clove, chopped

1 scallion, chopped

1 small fresh red chili, seeded
  and sliced

handful of cilantro

10½ oz/300 g dried fine egg noodles

2 tbsp vegetable oil

2 tsp sesame oil

1 tsp shrimp paste

8 oz/225 g raw shrimp, shelled

2 tbsp lime juice

2 tbsp Thai fish sauce

1 tsp sesame seeds, toasted

### COOK'S TIP

The roots of cilantro are widely
used in Thai cooking, so if you
can buy cilantro with the root
attached, the whole plant
can be used in this dish for
maximum flavor. If not, just
use the stems and leaves.

1 Place the garlic, onion, chili, and cilantro in a mortar and, using a pestle, grind to a smooth paste.

2 Drop the noodles into a pan of boiling water and return to a boil, then simmer for 4 minutes, or according to the package directions.

3 Meanwhile, heat the oils in a large skillet or preheated wok. Stir in the shrimp paste and ground cilantro mixture and stir over medium heat for 1 minute.

4 Stir in the shrimp and stir-fry for 2 minutes. Stir in the lime juice and fish sauce and cook for an additional 1 minute.

5 Drain the noodles and toss them into the skillet. Sprinkle with the toasted sesame seeds and serve immediately.

# hot & sour noodle salad

### serves four

12 oz/350 g rice vermicelli noodles

4 tbsp sesame oil

3 tbsp soy sauce

juice of 2 limes

1 tsp sugar

4 scallions, finely sliced

1–2 tsp hot chili sauce

2 tbsp chopped cilantro

1 Prepare the noodles according to the package directions. Drain, then toss with half the oil.

2 Mix the remaining oil, soy sauce, lime juice, sugar, scallions, and chili sauce together in a bowl. Stir into the noodles.

3 Stir in the chopped cilantro and serve immediately.

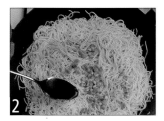

# fried egg noodles

## serves four

9 oz/250 g dried fine egg noodles

2 tbsp vegetable oil

2 garlic cloves, crushed

1 tbsp Thai fish sauce

3 tbsp lime juice

1 tsp sugar

2 eggs, lightly beaten

4 oz/115 g cooked, shelled shrimp

¾ cup fresh bean sprouts

6 scallions, finely sliced

TO GARNISH

2 tbsp finely chopped
roasted peanuts

handful of cilantro leaves

lime slices

1 Prepare the noodles according to the package directions. Drain, then rinse and drain again. Reserve.

2 Heat the oil in a preheated wok. Add the garlic and cook, stirring, for 1 minute, or until lightly browned but not burned. Stir in the fish sauce, lime juice, and sugar and stir until the sugar has dissolved.

3 Quickly stir in the eggs and cook for a few seconds. Stir in the noodles to coat with the garlic and eggs. Add the shrimp, bean sprouts, and half the scallions.

4 When everything is heated through, transfer the mixture to a warmed serving dish. Sprinkle the remaining scallions on top and serve, garnished with peanuts, cilantro leaves, and lime slices.

# rice noodles with chicken & napa cabbage

## serves four

7 oz/200 g rice stick noodles

1 tbsp corn oil

1 garlic clove, finely chopped

¾-inch/2-cm piece fresh gingerroot, finely chopped

4 scallions, chopped

1 fresh red Thai chili, seeded and sliced

10½ oz/300 g skinless, boneless chicken, finely chopped

2 chicken livers, finely chopped

1 celery stalk, thinly sliced

1 carrot, cut into fine short sticks

10½ oz/300 g shredded Napa cabbage

4 tbsp lime juice

2 tbsp Thai fish sauce

1 tbsp soy sauce

2 tbsp shredded fresh mint

slices of pickled garlic

fresh mint sprigs, to garnish

2 Heat the oil in a large skillet or preheated wok. Add the garlic, ginger, scallions, and chili and stir-fry for 1 minute. Stir in the chicken and chicken livers and stir-fry over high heat for 2–3 minutes, or until beginning to brown.

3 Stir in the celery and carrot and stir-fry for 2 minutes to soften. Add the Napa cabbage, then stir in the lime juice, fish sauce, and soy sauce.

1 Place the rice noodles in a bowl. Cover with hot water and let soak for 15 minutes, or according to the package directions. Drain well.

4 Add the noodles and stir to heat thoroughly. Sprinkle with shredded mint and pickled garlic. Serve immediately, garnished with mint sprigs.

# hot & sour noodles

## serves four

9 oz/250 g dried medium
   egg noodles

1 tbsp sesame oil

1 tbsp chili oil

1 garlic clove, crushed

2 scallions, finely chopped

1 cup sliced white mushrooms

1½ oz/40 g dried shiitake
   mushrooms, soaked, drained,
   and sliced

2 tbsp lime juice

3 tbsp light soy sauce

1 tsp sugar

TO SERVE

shredded Napa cabbage

2 tbsp shredded cilantro

2 tbsp toasted peanuts,
   chopped

1 Cook the noodles in a large pan of boiling water for 3–4 minutes, or according to the package directions. Drain well and return to the pan, then toss with the sesame oil and reserve.

2 Heat the chili oil in a large skillet or preheated wok. Add the garlic, scallions, and white mushrooms and quickly stir-fry to soften them.

3 Add the shiitake mushrooms, lime juice, soy sauce, and sugar and continue stir-frying until boiling. Add the noodles and toss to mix.

4 Arrange the noodles on a bed of Napa cabbage. Sprinkle with cilantro and peanuts and serve.

### COOK'S TIP

Thai chili oil is very hot, so if you want a milder flavor, use vegetable oil for the initial cooking instead, then add a final dribble of chili oil just for seasoning.

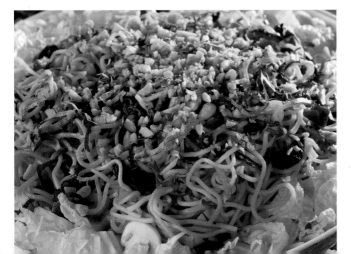

# drunken noodles

## serves four

6 oz/175 g rice stick noodles

2 tbsp vegetable oil

1 garlic clove, crushed

2 small fresh green chilies, chopped

1 small onion, thinly sliced

scant 1½ cups ground lean pork
   or chicken

1 small green bell pepper, seeded
   and finely chopped

4 fresh kaffir lime leaves,
   finely shredded

1 tbsp dark soy sauce

1 tbsp light soy sauce

½ tsp sugar

1 tomato, cut into thin wedges

2 tbsp finely sliced fresh
   basil leaves

1 Place the rice noodles in a bowl. Cover with hot water and let soak for 15 minutes, or according to the package directions. Drain well.

2 Heat the oil in a large skillet or preheated wok. Add the garlic, chilies, and onion and stir-fry for 1 minute.

3 Stir in the pork and stir-fry over high heat for an additional 1 minute, then add the bell pepper and continue stir-frying for an additional 2 minutes.

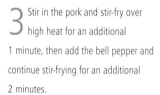

4 Stir in the lime leaves, soy sauces, and sugar. Add the noodles and tomato and toss well to heat thoroughly. Sprinkle with the basil and serve hot.

# pad thai noodles

## serves four

9 oz/250 g rice stick noodles

3 tbsp peanut oil

3 garlic cloves, finely chopped

4½ oz/125 g pork fillet, chopped
 into ¼-inch/5-mm pieces

7 oz/200 g cooked, shelled shrimp

1 tbsp sugar

3 tbsp Thai fish sauce

1 tbsp tomato ketchup

1 tbsp lime juice

2 eggs, beaten

generous ¾ cup fresh bean sprouts

TO GARNISH

1 tsp dried red chili flakes

2 scallions, thickly sliced

2 tbsp chopped cilantro

1 Place the rice noodles in a bowl. Cover with hot water and let soak for 15 minutes, or according to the package directions. Drain well and reserve until required.

2 Heat the oil in a large skillet. Add the garlic and cook over high heat for 30 seconds. Add the pork and stir-fry for 2–3 minutes, or until browned.

3 Stir in the shrimp, then add the sugar, fish sauce, ketchup, and lime juice and continue stir-frying for an additional 30 seconds.

4 Stir in the eggs and stir-fry until lightly set. Stir in the reserved noodles, then add the bean sprouts and stir-fry for an additional 30 seconds.

5 Transfer to a serving dish, sprinkle with chili flakes, scallions, and cilantro, and serve.

# thai-style noodle röstis

1 Break the rice noodles into short pieces and place in a bowl. Cover with hot water and let soak for 4 minutes, or according to the package directions. Drain thoroughly and pat dry with paper towels. Stir the noodles, scallions, lemongrass, and coconut together.

2 Heat a small amount of oil until very hot in a heavy-bottom skillet. Brush a 3½-inch/9-cm round cookie cutter with oil and place in the skillet. Spoon a small amount of noodle mixture into the cutter to just cover the bottom of the skillet, then press down with the back of a spoon.

3 Cook for 30 seconds, then carefully remove the cutter and continue cooking the rösti until golden brown, turning it over once. Remove and drain on paper towels. Repeat with the remaining noodles, to make 12 röstis.

4 To finish, arrange the noodle röstis in small stacks, with bean sprouts, onion, and avocado between the layers. Mix the lime juice, rice wine, and chili sauce together and spoon over just before serving, garnished with whole red chilies.

# rice noodles with spinach

## serves four

4 oz/115 g thin rice stick noodles

2 tbsp dried shrimp (optional)

9 oz/250 g fresh young spinach
  leaves

1 tbsp peanut oil

2 garlic cloves, finely chopped

2 tsp Thai green curry paste

1 tsp sugar

1 tbsp light soy sauce

### COOK'S TIP

It is best to choose young
spinach leaves for this dish
because they are beautifully
tender and cook within a matter
of seconds. If you can only get
older spinach, however, shred
the leaves before adding to the
dish so they cook more quickly.

1 Place the noodles in a bowl, then cover with hot water and let soak for 15 minutes, or according to the package directions. Drain well.

2 Place the shrimp, if using, in a bowl, then cover with hot water and let soak for 10 minutes. Drain well. Wash the spinach thoroughly, then drain well and remove any tough stems.

3 Heat the oil in a large skillet or preheated wok. Add the garlic and stir-fry for 1 minute. Stir in the curry paste and stir-fry for 30 seconds. Stir in the soaked shrimp, if using, and stir-fry for 30 seconds.

4 Add the spinach and stir-fry for 1–2 minutes, or until the leaves are just wilted.

5 Stir in the sugar and soy sauce, then add the noodles and toss thoroughly to mix evenly. Serve immediately while hot.

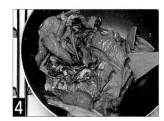

# crispy duck with noodles & tamarind

## serves four

3 duck breasts, about 14 oz/400 g
   in total

2 garlic cloves, crushed

1½ tsp chili paste

1 tbsp clear honey

3 tbsp dark soy sauce

½ tsp Chinese five-spice powder

9 oz/250 g rice stick noodles

1 tsp vegetable oil

1 tsp sesame oil

2 scallions, sliced

1 cup snow peas

2 tbsp tamarind juice

sesame seeds, for sprinkling

1 Prick the duck breast skin all over with a fork and place in a deep dish.

2 Mix the garlic, chili paste, honey, soy sauce, and five-spice powder together, then pour over the duck. Turn the breasts over to coat evenly, then cover and let marinate in the refrigerator for at least 1 hour.

3 Meanwhile, place the rice noodles in a bowl. Cover with hot water and let soak for 15 minutes. Drain well.

4 Preheat the broiler to high. Drain the duck breasts from the marinade, reserving it, and place on a broiler rack. Cook under the preheated broiler for 10 minutes, turning the duck breasts over occasionally, until golden brown. Remove and slice the duck breasts thinly.

5 Heat the oils in a skillet. Add the scallions and snow peas and toss for 2 minutes. Stir in the reserved marinade and tamarind juice and bring to a boil.

6 Add the sliced duck and noodles and toss to heat thoroughly. Serve immediately, sprinkled with sesame seeds.

# spicy fried rice

## serves four

1¼ cups long-grain rice

¼ oz/10 g dried mushrooms

2 tbsp vegetable oil

2 eggs, lightly beaten

2 garlic cloves, finely chopped

1 fresh red chili, seeded and
finely chopped

½-inch/1-cm piece fresh gingerroot,
finely grated

2 tbsp soy sauce

1 tsp sugar

2 tsp Thai fish sauce

6 scallions, finely chopped

1 lb/450 g cooked, shelled
small shrimp

14 oz/400 g canned baby corn
cobs, drained and cut in half

3 tbsp chopped cilantro

1 Place the rice in a strainer and rinse under cold running water. Drain thoroughly. Add the rice to a large pan of boiling salted water, then return to a boil and cook for 10 minutes, or until tender. Drain, then rinse and drain again.

2 Place the mushrooms in a bowl, then cover with warm water and let stand for 20 minutes. Drain and cut into slices.

3 Heat half the oil in a preheated wok. Add the eggs. Stir the uncooked egg to the outside edge of the wok. Cook until firm. Remove the omelet, then roll up and cut into strips.

### COOK'S TIP

It is important to rinse the rice under cold running water, because this removes the excess starch. If you have time, wash the rice in several changes of water until the water is clear. Drain well.

4 Heat the remaining oil in the wok. Add the garlic, chili, and ginger and cook for 1 minute. Add the soy sauce, sugar, fish sauce, and scallions, stirring to dissolve the sugar. Stir in the reserved rice, shrimp, and corn cobs, tossing to mix. Cook for 3–4 minutes, or until the rice is heated through. Stir in the cilantro, then turn into a warmed serving bowl and serve.

# jasmine rice with lemon & basil

### serves four

scant 2 cups jasmine rice

3¼ cups water

finely grated rind of ½ lemon

2 tbsp shredded fresh basil

---

### COOK'S TIP

It is important to leave the pan tightly covered while the rice cooks and steams inside, so the grains cook evenly and become fluffy and separate.

1 Wash the rice in several changes of cold water until the water runs clear. Bring 3¼ cups of water to a boil in a large pan, then add the rice.

2 Return to a rolling boil. Turn the heat to a low simmer, then cover the pan and simmer for an additional 12 minutes.

3 Remove the pan from the heat and let stand, covered, for 10 minutes.

4 Fluff up the rice with a fork, then stir in the lemon rind. Serve sprinkled with shredded basil.

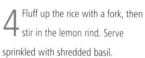

# egg noodle salad with lime & basil dressing

## serves four

8 oz/225 g dried egg noodles

2 tsp sesame oil

1 carrot

scant ⅔ cup fresh bean sprouts

½ cucumber

2 scallions, finely shredded

5½ oz/150 g cooked turkey breast
   meat, shredded into thin slivers

chopped peanuts, for sprinkling

fresh basil leaves, to garnish

DRESSING

5 tbsp coconut milk

3 tbsp lime juice

1 tbsp light soy sauce

2 tsp Thai fish sauce

1 tsp chili oil

1 tsp sugar

2 tbsp chopped cilantro

2 tbsp chopped fresh basil

1 Cook the noodles in boiling water for 4 minutes, or according to the package directions. Plunge them into a bowl of cold water to cool, then drain and toss in the sesame oil.

2 Use a vegetable peeler to shave off thin ribbons from the carrot. Blanch the ribbons and bean sprouts in boiling water for 30 seconds, then plunge into cold water for 30 seconds. Drain well. Shave thin ribbons of cucumber with the vegetable peeler.

3 Toss the carrot, bean sprouts, cucumber, and scallions together with the turkey and noodles.

4 Place all the dressing ingredients in a screw-top jar and shake well to mix evenly.

5 Add the dressing to the noodle mixture and toss. Pile on to a serving dish. Sprinkle with peanuts and garnish with basil leaves. Serve cold.

# coconut rice with pineapple

## serves four

1 cup long-grain rice

generous 2 cups coconut milk

2 lemongrass stems

generous ¾ cup water

2 slices fresh pineapple, peeled
and diced

2 tbsp toasted coconut

chili sauce, to serve

---

### VARIATION

A sweet version of this dish
can be made by simply omitting
the lemongrass and stirring
in palm sugar or superfine
sugar to taste during cooking.
Serve as a dessert, with extra
pineapple slices.

---

1 Wash the rice in several changes of cold water until the water runs clear. Place in a large pan with the coconut milk.

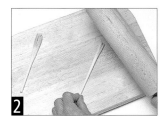

2 Place the lemongrass on a counter and bruise it by hitting firmly with a rolling pin or mallet. Add to the pan with the rice and coconut milk.

3 Add the water and bring to a boil. Reduce the heat, then cover the pan tightly and simmer gently for 15 minutes. Remove the pan from the heat and fluff up the rice with a fork.

4 Remove the lemongrass and stir in the pineapple. Sprinkle with toasted coconut and serve immediately with chili sauce.

158

# stir-fried rice with egg strips

## serves four

2 tbsp peanut oil

1 egg, beaten with 1 tsp water

1 garlic clove, finely chopped

1 small onion, finely chopped

1 tbsp Thai red curry paste

1¼ cups long-grain rice, cooked

½ cup cooked peas

1 tbsp Thai fish sauce

2 tbsp tomato ketchup

2 tbsp chopped cilantro

TO GARNISH

fresh red chili flowers

cucumber slices

### COOK'S TIP

Many Thai rice dishes are made from leftover rice that has been cooked for an earlier meal. Nothing goes to waste and it's often stir-fried with a few simple ingredients and aromatic flavorings, as in this recipe. If you have any leftover vegetables or meat, this is a good way to use them up.

1 To make chili flowers for the garnish, hold the stem of a fresh red chili with your fingertips and use a small, sharp, pointed knife to cut a slit down the length from near the stem end to the tip. Turn the chili about a quarter turn and make another cut. Repeat to make a total of 4 cuts, then scrape out the seeds. Cut each "petal" again in half, or into fourths, to make 8–16 petals. Place the chili flower in ice water.

2 Heat 1 teaspoon of the oil in a preheated wok or large skillet. Pour in the egg mixture, swirling it to coat the wok evenly and make a thin layer. When set and golden, remove the egg from the wok and roll up. Reserve until required.

3 Add the remaining oil to the wok. Add the garlic and onion and stir-fry for 1 minute. Add the curry paste, then stir in the rice and peas.

4 Stir in the fish sauce, ketchup, and cilantro. Remove the wok from the heat and pile the rice on to a serving dish. Slice the egg roll into spiral strips, without unrolling, and use to garnish the rice. Add the cucumber slices and chili flowers. Serve hot.

# rice with seafood

## serves four

12 live mussels in shells

8 cups fish stock

2 tbsp vegetable oil

1 garlic clove, crushed

1 tsp grated fresh gingerroot

1 fresh red Thai chili, chopped

2 scallions, chopped

generous 1 cup long-grain rice

2 small squid, cleaned and sliced

3½ oz/100 g firm white fish fillet,
  such as halibut or angler fish,
  cut into chunks

3½ oz/100 g raw shrimp, shelled

2 tbsp Thai fish sauce

3 tbsp shredded cilantro,
  for sprinkling

1 Clean the mussels thoroughly by scrubbing or scraping the shells and pulling out any beards that are attached to them. Discard any mussels with broken shells or any that refuse to close when firmly tapped. Heat 4 tablespoons of the stock in a large pan. Add the mussels and cook, covered, over a high heat for 3–4 minutes, shaking the pan occasionally, until the mussels have opened. Remove the pan from the heat and discard any mussels that remain closed.

2 Heat the oil in a large skillet or preheated wok. Add the garlic, ginger, chili, and scallions and stir-fry for 30 seconds. Add the remaining stock and bring to a boil.

3 Stir in the rice, then add the squid, white fish, and shrimp. Reduce the heat and simmer gently for 15 minutes, or until the rice is cooked. Add the fish sauce and mussels.

4 Ladle into wide bowls and sprinkle with shredded cilantro before serving.

### VARIATION

You could use leftover cooked rice for this dish. Just simmer the seafood gently until cooked, then stir in the rice at the end.

# Vegetables & Salads

Many of the vegetables, salad greens, and shoots that Thais use in cooking are native, often growing wild locally. This makes it difficult to produce authentic Thai salads at home.

You may have to substitute a few fresh ingredients with canned ones, but luckily you can now buy a good selection of cultivated Asian vegetables, such as bok choy and Napa cabbage.

A Thai salad can make a stunning centerpiece for any dinner table. Thai cooks usually add strips of finely chopped cooked meat, fish, or shellfish to their salads, or for vegetarian dishes, mushrooms or tofu are added.

Dressings are typically piquant and spicy, with the skillful balance of bitter, salt, sour, hot, and sweet tastes. To finish, a sprinkling of peanuts or dried chilies, chopped cilantro, and a final flourish of chili flowers add color.

# crisp pickled vegetables

### serves six–eight

½ small cauliflower

½ cucumber

2 carrots

generous 1½ cups green beans

½ small Napa cabbage

generous 2 cups rice vinegar or
   white wine vinegar

1 tbsp superfine sugar

1 tsp salt

3 garlic cloves

3 shallots

3 fresh red Thai chilies, seeded

5 tbsp peanut oil

1 Trim the cauliflower. Peel and seed the cucumber. Peel the carrots. Trim the beans. Trim the cabbage, then cut all the vegetables into bite-size pieces.

2 Place the rice vinegar, sugar, and salt in a large, heavy-bottom pan and bring almost to a boil. Add the vegetables, then reduce the heat and simmer for 3–4 minutes, or until they are just tender but still crisp inside. Remove the pan from the heat and let the vegetables and vinegar cool.

3 Place the garlic, shallots, and chilies in a mortar and, using a pestle, grind to a smooth paste.

---

**COOK'S TIP**

To make simple carrot flowers, peel the carrot thinly as usual, then use a stripper or small sharp knife to cut narrow "channels" down the length of it at regular intervals. Slice the carrot as usual, and the slices will resemble flowers.

---

4 Heat the oil in a skillet. Add the spice paste and stir-fry gently for 1–2 minutes. Add the vegetables with the vinegar and cook for an additional 2 minutes to reduce the liquid slightly. Remove the skillet from the heat and let cool.

5 Serve the pickles cold, or pack into jars and store in the refrigerator for up to 2 weeks.

# stir-fried green vegetables

## serves four

generous 1 cup snow peas

2 tbsp vegetable oil

3 garlic cloves, thinly sliced

1-inch/2.5-cm piece fresh
   gingerroot, thinly sliced

6 oz/175 g fresh young spinach
   leaves, washed and drained

6 oz/175 g broccoli, cut into
   small florets

¾ cup green beans, halved

pepper

1 tbsp Thai fish sauce

1 tbsp oyster sauce

1 tsp sugar

4 scallions, diagonally chopped

1 Cut the snow peas in half. Heat
  the oil in a preheated wok. Add
the garlic and ginger and cook for
1 minute. Add the spinach, broccoli,
and beans and cook for 2 minutes.

2 Add the snow peas to the wok
  and stir-fry over high heat for
2 minutes.

3 Add pepper to taste, fish sauce,
  oyster sauce, sugar, and scallions
and stir-fry for an additional 2 minutes.

4 Transfer to a warmed serving
  plate and serve.

# spiced cashew nut curry

## serves four

1⅔ cups unsalted cashew nuts

1 tsp coriander seeds

1 tsp cumin seeds

2 cardamom pods, crushed

1 tbsp corn oil

1 onion, finely sliced

1 garlic clove, crushed

1 small fresh green chili, seeded
   and chopped

1 cinnamon stick

½ tsp ground turmeric

4 tbsp coconut cream

1¼ cups hot vegetable stock

3 dried kaffir lime leaves,
   crumbled

cilantro leaves, to garnish

freshly cooked jasmine rice, to serve

1 Place the cashew nuts in a bowl, then cover with cold water and let soak overnight. Drain thoroughly. Crush the seeds and cardamom pods in a mortar using a pestle.

2 Heat the oil in a large skillet. Add the onion and garlic and stir-fry for 2–3 minutes to soften but not brown. Add the chili, crushed spices, cinnamon stick, and turmeric and stir-fry for an additional 1 minute.

3 Add the coconut cream and the hot stock to the skillet. Bring to a boil, then add the cashew nuts and lime leaves.

4 Cover the skillet, then reduce the heat and simmer for 20 minutes. Serve hot with jasmine rice garnished with cilantro leaves.

## COOK'S TIP

All spices give the best flavor when freshly crushed, but if you prefer, you can use ready-ground spices instead of crushing them yourself in a mortar.

# mixed vegetables in peanut sauce

2 carrots

1 small cauliflower, trimmed

2 small heads green bok choy

1 cup green beans

2 tbsp vegetable oil

1 garlic clove, finely chopped

6 scallions, sliced

1 tsp chili paste

2 tbsp soy sauce

2 tbsp rice wine or dry sherry

4 tbsp smooth peanut butter

3 tbsp coconut milk

TO GARNISH

1 whole fresh red chili

scallion curls (see page 212)

---

### COOK'S TIP

It's important to cut the vegetables thinly into even-size pieces so they cook quickly and evenly. Prepare all the vegetables before you begin to cook.

---

1 Cut the carrots diagonally into thin slices. Cut the cauliflower into small florets, then slice the stem thinly. Thickly slice the bok choy. Cut the beans into 1¼-inch/3-cm lengths.

2 Heat the oil in a large skillet or preheated wok. Add the garlic and scallions and stir-fry for 1 minute. Stir in the chili paste and cook for a few seconds.

3 Add the carrots and cauliflower and stir-fry for 2–3 minutes.

4 Add the bok choy and beans and stir-fry for an additional 2 minutes. Stir in the soy sauce and rice wine.

5 Mix the peanut butter with the coconut milk and stir into the skillet, then cook, stirring, for an additional 1 minute. Transfer to a serving dish and garnish with a red chili and scallion curls. Serve hot.

# stir-fried ginger mushrooms

## serves four

2 tbsp vegetable oil

3 garlic cloves, crushed

1 tbsp Thai red curry paste

½ tsp ground turmeric

15 oz/425 g canned straw
    mushrooms, drained and halved

¾-inch/2-cm piece fresh gingerroot,
    finely shredded

scant ½ cup coconut milk

1½ oz/40 g dried shiitake
    mushrooms, soaked, drained,
    and sliced

1 tbsp lemon juice

1 tbsp light soy sauce

2 tsp sugar

½ tsp salt

8 cherry tomatoes, halved

7 oz/200 g firm tofu (drained
    weight), diced cilantro leaves,
    for sprinkling

scallion curls, to garnish (see
    page 212)

freshly cooked Thai fragrant rice,
    to serve

1 Heat the oil in a preheated wok or large skillet. Add the garlic and cook for 1 minute, stirring. Stir in the curry paste and turmeric and cook for an additional 30 seconds.

2 Stir in the straw mushrooms and ginger and stir-fry for 2 minutes. Stir in the coconut milk and bring to a boil.

3 Stir in the shiitake mushrooms, lemon juice, soy sauce, sugar, and salt and heat thoroughly. Add the tomatoes and tofu and toss gently to heat through.

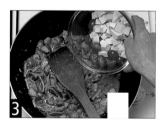

4 Sprinkle the cilantro over the mixture and serve hot with freshly cooked fragrant rice garnished with scallion curls.

### VARIATION

You can vary the mushrooms depending on your own taste—try a mixture of oyster with the shiitake for a change. Even just ordinary cultivated white mushrooms are delicious cooked in this way.

# spiced mushrooms

## serves four

8 large flat mushrooms

3 tbsp corn oil

2 tbsp light soy sauce

1 garlic clove, crushed

¾-inch/2-cm piece fresh galangal or gingerroot, grated

1 tbsp Thai green curry paste

8 baby corn cobs, sliced

3 scallions, chopped

generous ¾ cup fresh bean sprouts

3½ oz/100 g firm tofu (drained weight), diced

2 tsp sesame seeds, toasted

TO SERVE

chopped cucumber

sliced red bell pepper

1 Preheat the broiler to high. Remove the stems from the mushrooms and reserve. Place the caps on a baking sheet. Mix 2 tablespoons of the oil with 1 tablespoon of the soy sauce and brush over the mushrooms.

2 Cook the mushroom caps under the hot broiler until golden and tender, turning them over once.

3 Meanwhile, chop the mushroom stems finely. Heat the remaining oil in a large skillet or preheated wok. Add the stems, garlic, and galangal and stir-fry for 1 minute.

4 Stir in the curry paste, baby corn cobs, and scallions and stir-fry for 1 minute. Add the bean sprouts and stir for an additional 1 minute.

5 Add the diced tofu and remaining soy sauce, then toss lightly to heat. Spoon the mixture into the mushroom caps.

6 Sprinkle with sesame seeds and serve with chopped cucumber and sliced red bell pepper.

### COOK'S TIP

Galangal or ginger can be frozen for several weeks, either peeled and finely chopped ready to add to dishes, or in whole pieces. Thaw the piece or grate finely from frozen.

# roasted spiced bell peppers

## serves four

2 red bell peppers

2 yellow bell peppers

2 green bell peppers

2 fresh red Thai chilies, seeded and
finely chopped

1 lemongrass stem, finely shredded

4 tbsp lime juice

2 tbsp palm sugar

1 tbsp Thai fish sauce

### COOK'S TIP

The flavors will mingle best if the
bell peppers are still slightly
warm when you spoon the
dressing over. Prepare the
dressing while the bell peppers
are cooking, so it's ready to pour
over when they are cooked.

1 Preheat the broiler or grill or the
oven to 350°F/180°C. Roast the
bell peppers under the hot broiler, grill
over hot coals, or roast in the oven,
turning them over occasionally, until
the skins are charred. Let cool slightly,
then remove the skins. Cut each in half
and remove the core and seeds.

2 Slice the bell peppers thickly and
transfer to a large bowl.

3 Place the chilies, lemongrass, lime
juice, sugar, and fish sauce in a
screw-top jar and shake well until
thoroughly mixed.

4 Pour the dressing evenly over the
peppers. Let cool completely, then
cover with plastic wrap and let chill in
the refrigerator for at least 1 hour
before serving. Transfer to a serving
dish to serve.

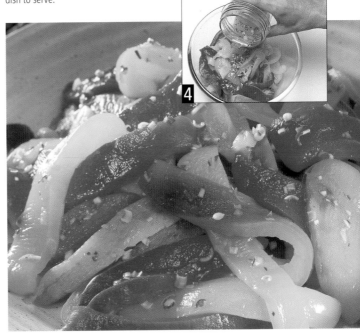

# sweet potato cakes with soy-tomato sauce

## serves four

2 sweet potatoes, 1 lb 2 oz/500 g
in total
2 garlic cloves, crushed
1 small fresh green chili, chopped
2 cilantro sprigs, chopped
1 tbsp dark soy sauce
all-purpose flour, for dusting
vegetable oil, for pan-frying
sesame seeds, for sprinkling
cilantro sprigs, to garnish
SOY-TOMATO SAUCE
2 tsp vegetable oil
1 garlic clove, finely chopped
¾-inch/2-cm piece fresh gingerroot,
finely chopped
3 tomatoes, skinned and chopped
2 tbsp dark soy sauce
1 tbsp lime juice
2 tbsp chopped cilantro

1 To make the soy-tomato sauce, heat the oil in a preheated wok. Add the garlic and ginger and stir-fry for 1 minute. Add the tomatoes and stir-fry for an additional 2 minutes. Remove the wok from the heat and stir in the soy sauce, lime juice, and cilantro. Keep warm.

2 Peel the sweet potatoes and grate finely (you can do this quickly in a food processor). Place the garlic, chili, and cilantro in a mortar and, using a pestle, grind to a smooth paste. Stir in the soy sauce and mix with the grated sweet potatoes.

3 Spread the flour out on a plate. Divide the mixture into 12 equal portions, then dip into the flour and pat into flat, round patty shapes.

4 Heat a shallow layer of oil in a wide skillet. Cook the sweet potato patties over high heat until golden, turning once.

5 Drain on paper towels and sprinkle with sesame seeds. Transfer to a large serving plate, then garnish with cilantro sprigs and serve hot with the soy-tomato sauce.

# chili & coconut sambal

## serves six–eight

1 small coconut

1 slice fresh pineapple, finely diced

1 small onion, finely chopped

2 small fresh green chilies, seeded
and chopped

2-inch/5-cm piece lemongrass,
chopped

½ tsp salt

1 tsp shrimp paste

1 tbsp lime juice

2 tbsp chopped cilantro

cilantro sprigs, to garnish

### VARIATION

To make a quicker version of this
sambal, stir 1 teaspoon of Thai
green curry paste into freshly
grated coconut and add finely
diced pineapple and lime
juice to taste.

1 Puncture 2 of the coconut "eyes"
with a screwdriver and pour the
milk out from the shell. Crack the
coconut open, then prize away the
flesh and coarsely grate it into a bowl.

2 Mix the coconut with the
pineapple, onion, chilies, and
lemongrass.

3 Blend the salt, shrimp paste, and
lime juice together in a separate
bowl, then stir into the sambal.

4 Stir in the cilantro. Spoon into a
small serving dish and garnish
with cilantro sprigs.

# sweet & sour potato stir-fry

## serves four

4 waxy potatoes, diced

2 tbsp vegetable oil

1 yellow bell pepper, diced

1 red bell pepper, diced

1 carrot, cut into short thin sticks

1 zucchini, cut into short thin sticks

2 garlic cloves, crushed

1 fresh red chili, sliced

1 bunch of scallions,
    halved lengthwise

8 tbsp coconut milk

1 tsp chopped lemongrass

2 tsp lime juice

finely grated rind of 1 lime

1 tbsp chopped cilantro

### COOK'S TIP

Check that the potatoes are not overcooked in step 1, otherwise the potato pieces will disintegrate when they are stir-fried in the wok.

1 Cook the diced potatoes in a pan of boiling water for 5 minutes. Drain thoroughly.

2 Heat the oil in a preheated wok or large skillet. Add the potatoes, diced bell peppers, carrot, zucchini, garlic, and chili and stir-fry for 2–3 minutes.

3 Stir in the scallions, coconut milk, chopped lemongrass, and lime juice and stir-fry for an additional 5 minutes.

4 Add the lime rind and cilantro and stir-fry for 1 minute. Serve hot.

### VARIATION

Almost any combination of vegetables is suitable for this dish; the yellow and red bell peppers, for example, can be replaced with crisp green beans or snow peas.

# potatoes in creamed coconut

## serves four

1 lb 5 oz/600 g potatoes

1 onion, thinly sliced

2 fresh red Thai chilies,
   finely chopped

½ tsp salt

½ tsp pepper

3 oz/85 g creamed coconut

1½ cups vegetable or chicken stock

cilantro or fresh basil, chopped,
   to garnish

1 Peel the potatoes, then using a sharp knife, cut them into ¾-inch/ 2-cm chunks.

2 Place the potatoes in a pan with the onion, chilies, salt, pepper, and creamed coconut. Stir in the stock.

3 Bring to a boil, stirring constantly. Reduce the heat, then cover and simmer gently, stirring occasionally, until the potatoes are tender.

4 Adjust the seasoning to taste if necessary, then sprinkle with chopped cilantro or basil. Serve hot.

### COOK'S TIP

If the potatoes are a thin-skinned, or a new variety, simply wash or scrub to remove any dirt and cook with the skins on. This adds extra nutrients to the finished dish, and cuts down on the preparation time. Baby new potatoes can be cooked whole.

# potato & spinach yellow curry

## serves four

2 garlic cloves, finely chopped

1¼-inch/3-cm piece fresh galangal, finely chopped

1 lemongrass stem, finely chopped

1 tsp coriander seeds

3 tbsp vegetable oil

2 tsp Thai red curry paste

½ tsp ground turmeric

generous ¾ cup coconut milk

9 oz/250 g potatoes, cut into ¾-inch/2-cm cubes

scant ½ cup vegetable stock

7 oz/200 g fresh young spinach leaves

1 small onion, thinly sliced

1 Place the garlic, galangal, lemongrass, and coriander seeds in a mortar and, using a pestle, grind to a smooth paste.

2 Heat 2 tablespoons of the oil in a skillet or preheated wok. Stir in the garlic paste mixture and stir-fry for 30 seconds. Stir in the curry paste and turmeric, then add the coconut milk and bring to a boil.

3 Add the potatoes and stock. Return to a boil, then reduce the heat and simmer, uncovered, for 10–12 minutes, or until the potatoes are almost tender.

4 Stir in the spinach and simmer until the leaves are wilted.

5 Meanwhile, heat the remaining oil in a separate skillet. Add the onion and cook until crisp and golden brown.

6 Place the fried onions on top of the curry just before serving.

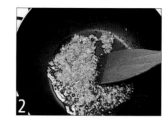

# red bean curry

## serves four

14 oz/400 g green beans

1 garlic clove, finely sliced

1 fresh red Thai chili, seeded
and chopped

½ tsp paprika

1 piece lemongrass stem,
finely chopped

2 tsp Thai fish sauce

½ cup coconut milk

1 tbsp corn oil

2 scallions, sliced

---

### VARIATION

Young string beans can be used
instead of green beans. Remove
any strings from the beans, then
cut at a diagonal angle in short
lengths. Cook as in the recipe
until tender.

---

1 Cut the beans into 2-inch/5-cm
pieces and cook in boiling water
for 2 minutes. Drain well.

2 Place the garlic, chili, paprika,
lemongrass, fish sauce, and
coconut milk in a food processor and
process to a smooth paste.

3 Heat the oil in a large skillet or
preheated wok. Add the scallions
and stir-fry over high heat for 1 minute.
Add the paste and bring the mixture
to a boil.

4 Simmer for 3–4 minutes to reduce
the liquid by about half. Add
the beans and simmer for an additional
1–2 minutes, or until tender. Transfer
to a serving dish and serve hot.

# vegetable & coconut curry

## serves four

2 lb 4 oz/1 kg mixed vegetables

1 onion, coarsely chopped

3 garlic cloves, thinly sliced

1-inch/2.5-cm piece fresh
    gingerroot, thinly sliced

2 fresh green chilies, seeded
    and finely chopped

1 tbsp vegetable oil

1 tsp ground turmeric

1 tsp ground coriander

1 tsp ground cumin

7 oz/200 g creamed coconut

2½ cups boiling water

salt and pepper

2 tbsp chopped cilantro,
    to garnish

freshly cooked rice, to serve

1 Cut the mixed vegetables into chunks. Place the onion, garlic, ginger, and chilies in a food processor and process until almost smooth.

2 Heat the oil in a large, heavy-bottom skillet. Add the onion mixture and cook for 5 minutes.

3 Add the turmeric, coriander, and cumin and cook for 3–4 minutes, stirring. Add the mixed vegetables and stir to coat in the spice paste.

4 Mix the creamed coconut and boiling water together in a pitcher. Stir until the coconut has dissolved. Add the coconut milk to the vegetables, then cover and simmer for 30–40 minutes, or until the vegetables are tender.

5 Season to taste with salt and pepper, then garnish with the chopped cilantro and serve with rice.

### COOK'S TIP
Use whatever vegetables you have to hand, such as cauliflower, zucchini, potatoes, carrots, and green beans.

# asian vegetables with yellow bean sauce

## serves four

1 eggplant

salt

2 tbsp vegetable oil

3 garlic cloves, crushed

4 scallions, chopped

1 small red bell pepper, seeded and
    thinly sliced

4 baby corn cobs, halved
    lengthwise

scant 1 cup snow peas

7 oz/200 g green bok choy,
    coarsely shredded

14½ oz/425 g canned straw
    mushrooms, drained

generous ¾ cup fresh bean sprouts

2 tbsp rice wine or dry sherry

2 tbsp yellow bean sauce

2 tbsp dark soy sauce

1 tsp chili sauce

1 tsp sugar

½ cup chicken or vegetable stock

1 tsp cornstarch

2 tsp water

1 Cut the eggplant into 2-inch/
5-cm long thin sticks. Place in a
colander, then sprinkle with salt and
let stand for 30 minutes. Rinse in cold
water and dry with paper towels.

2 Heat the oil in a skillet or
preheated wok. Add the garlic,
scallions, and bell pepper and stir-fry
over high heat for 1 minute. Stir in the
eggplant pieces and stir-fry for an
additional 1 minute, or until softened.

3 Stir in the corn cobs and snow
peas and stir-fry for 1 minute.
Add the bok choy, mushrooms,
and bean sprouts and stir-fry for
30 seconds.

4 Mix the rice wine, yellow bean
sauce, soy sauce, chili sauce, and
sugar together in a bowl, then add to
the skillet with the stock. Bring to a
boil, stirring constantly.

5 Slowly blend the cornstarch with
the water to form a smooth paste,
then stir quickly into the skillet
and cook for an additional 1 minute.
Serve immediately.

# crispy tofu with chili-soy sauce

## serves four

10½ oz/300 g firm tofu
  (drained weight)

2 tbsp vegetable oil

1 garlic clove, sliced

1 carrot, cut into short thin sticks

½ green bell pepper, seeded and cut
  into short thin sticks

1 fresh red Thai chili, seeded and
  finely chopped

2 tbsp soy sauce

1 tbsp lime juice

1 tbsp Thai fish sauce

1 tbsp brown sugar

pickled garlic slices, to serve
  (optional)

1 Drain the tofu and pat dry with paper towels. Cut the tofu into ¾-inch/2-cm cubes.

2 Heat the oil in a preheated wok or large skillet. Add the garlic and stir-fry for 1 minute. Remove the garlic and add the tofu, then cook quickly, turning gently to brown well on all sides.

3 Remove the tofu, then drain well and keep hot. Stir the carrot and bell pepper into the wok and stir-fry for 1 minute.

4 Transfer the carrot and bell pepper to a dish. Pile the tofu on top.

5 Mix the chili, soy sauce, lime juice, fish sauce, and sugar together in a bowl, stirring until the sugar is dissolved.

6 Spoon the sauce over the tofu and serve topped with pickled garlic slices, if using. Serve hot.

# stir-fried broccoli in oyster sauce

## serves four

14 oz/400 g broccoli

1 tbsp peanut oil

2 shallots, finely chopped

1 garlic clove, finely chopped

1 tbsp rice wine or dry sherry

5 tbsp oyster sauce

¼ tsp pepper

1 tsp chili oil

1 Cut the broccoli into small florets. Blanch in a pan of boiling water for 30 seconds, then drain well.

2 Heat the oil in a large skillet or preheated wok. Add the shallots and garlic and stir-fry for 1–2 minutes, or until golden brown.

3 Stir in the broccoli and stir-fry for 2 minutes. Add the rice wine and oyster sauce and stir for an additional 1 minute.

4 Stir in the pepper and drizzle with a little chili oil just before serving.

**COOK'S TIP**

To make chili oil, put fresh red or green chilies into a jar and top up with olive oil or a light vegetable oil. Cover with a lid and let infuse for at least 3 weeks before using.

# vegetable fritters with sweet chili dip

1 cup all-purpose flour

1 tsp ground coriander

1 tsp ground cumin

1 tsp ground turmeric

1 tsp salt

½ tsp pepper

2 garlic cloves, finely chopped

1¼-inch/3-cm piece fresh
   gingerroot, chopped

2 small fresh green chilies,
   finely chopped

1 tbsp chopped cilantro

scant 1 cup cold water

1 onion, chopped

1 potato, coarsely grated

¾ cup canned corn kernels

1 small eggplant, diced

4½ oz/125 g Chinese kale, cut into
   short lengths

coconut oil, for deep-frying

SWEET CHILI DIP

2 fresh red Thai chilies,
   finely chopped

4 tbsp superfine sugar

4 tbsp rice vinegar or white
   wine vinegar

1 tbsp light soy sauce

1 Make the dip by mixing all the ingredients together thoroughly until the sugar is dissolved. Cover and reserve until required.

2 To make the fritters, place the flour in a bowl and stir in the coriander, cumin, turmeric, salt, and pepper. Add the garlic, ginger, green chilies, and cilantro with just enough of the water to form a thick batter.

3 Add the onion, potato, corn kernels, eggplant, and broccoli to the batter and stir well to distribute the ingredients evenly.

4 Heat the oil in a deep skillet or wok to 350–375°F/180–190°C, or until a cube of bread browns in 30 seconds. Drop tablespoons of the batter into the hot oil and cook in batches until golden and crisp, turning once.

5 Drain the fritters well on paper towels and serve hot with the sweet chili dip.

# corn fritters

## serves four

generous ½ cup all-purpose flour

1 large egg

2 tsp Thai green curry paste

5 tbsp coconut milk

14 oz/400 g canned or frozen
   corn kernels

4 scallions

1 tbsp chopped cilantro

1 tbsp chopped fresh basil

salt and pepper

vegetable oil, for pan-frying

lime wedges, to garnish

chili relish, to serve

1 Place the flour, egg, curry paste, coconut milk, and about half the corn kernels in a food processor and process to a smooth, thick batter.

2 Finely chop the scallions and stir into the batter with the remaining corn, chopped cilantro, and basil. Season well with salt and pepper.

3 Heat a small amount of oil in a wide, heavy-bottom skillet. Drop in tablespoonfuls of the batter and cook for 2–3 minutes, or until golden brown.

4 Turn them over and cook for an additional 2–3 minutes, or until golden. Cook in batches, making 12–16 fritters, keeping the cooked fritters hot while you cook the remaining batter.

5 Transfer the fritters to a serving plate, then garnish with lime wedges and serve with a chili relish.

# bok choy with crabmeat

## serves four

2 heads green bok choy, about

    9 oz/250 g in total

2 tbsp vegetable oil

1 garlic clove, thinly sliced

2 tbsp oyster sauce

3½ oz/100 g cherry

    tomatoes, halved

6 oz/175 g canned white

    crabmeat, drained

salt and pepper

### VARIATION

For a vegetarian version of this dish, omit the crabmeat and replace the oyster sauce with 2 tablespoons of light soy sauce.

1 Using a sharp knife, cut the bok choy into 1-inch/2.5-cm thick slices.

2 Heat the oil in a large skillet or preheated wok. Add the garlic and stir-fry quickly over high heat for 1 minute.

3 Add the bok choy and stir-fry for 2–3 minutes, or until the leaves wilt but the stems are still crisp.

4 Add the oyster sauce and tomatoes and stir-fry for an additional 1 minute.

5 Add the crabmeat and season well with salt and pepper. Stir to heat thoroughly and break up the crabmeat before serving.

# bamboo shoot salad

## serves four

2 shallots, unpeeled

2 garlic cloves, unpeeled

2 tbsp Thai fish sauce

3 tbsp lime juice

½ tsp dried chili flakes

1 tsp granulated sugar

1 tbsp round-grain rice

2 tsp sesame seeds

12 oz/350 g canned bamboo
    shoots, drained

2 scallions, chopped

Napa cabbage or lettuce, shredded

fresh mint leaves, to garnish

1 Preheat the broiler to medium. Place the shallots and garlic under the hot broiler and cook until charred on the outside and tender inside. Let cool slightly, then remove the skins and discard. Place the flesh in a mortar and, using a pestle, grind to a smooth paste.

2 Mix the shallot and garlic paste with the fish sauce, lime juice, chili flakes, and sugar in a small bowl.

3 Place the rice and sesame seeds in a heavy-bottom skillet and cook to a rich golden brown color, shaking the skillet to brown evenly. Remove the skillet from the heat and let cool slightly. Crush the toasted rice and sesame seeds lightly in a mortar using a pestle.

4 Use a sharp knife to shred the bamboo shoots into short thin sticks and place in a bowl. Stir in the shallot and garlic dressing, tossing well to coat evenly. Stir in the toasted rice and sesame seeds, then the scallions.

5 Pile the salad on to a serving dish and surround with shredded Napa cabbage. Garnish with mint leaves and serve.

# asian lettuce cups

## serves four

8 leaves romaine lettuce, or similar
   firm lettuce leaves

2 carrots

2 celery stalks

3½ oz/100 g baby corn cobs

2 scallions

⅔ cup fresh bean sprouts

2 tbsp roasted peanuts, chopped

DRESSING

2 tbsp smooth peanut butter

3 tbsp lime juice

3 tbsp coconut milk

2 tsp Thai fish sauce

1 tsp superfine sugar

1 tsp grated fresh gingerroot

¼ tsp Thai red curry paste

1 Wash and trim the lettuce leaves, leaving them whole. Arrange on a serving plate or on individual plates.

2 Trim the carrots and celery and cut into short thin sticks. Trim the corn cobs and scallions and slice both diagonally.

3 Toss all the prepared vegetables together with the bean sprouts. Divide the salad mixture evenly between the individual lettuce cups.

### COOK'S TIP

Choose leaves with a deep cup shape to hold the salad neatly. If you prefer, Napa cabbage may be used in place of the romaine lettuce. To remove the leaves from the whole head without tearing them, cut a thick slice from the base end so the leaves are not attached by their stems, then gently ease away the leafy parts.

4 To make the dressing, place all the ingredients in a screw-top jar and shake well until thoroughly mixed.

5 Spoon the dressing evenly over the salad cups and sprinkle with chopped peanuts. Serve immediately.

# eggplant & mushroom stuffed omelet

## serves four

3 tbsp vegetable oil

1 garlic clove, finely chopped

1 small onion, finely chopped

1 small eggplant, diced

½ small green bell pepper, seeded
  and chopped

1 large dried shiitake mushroom,
  soaked, drained, and sliced

1 tomato, diced

1 tbsp light soy sauce

½ tsp sugar

¼ tsp pepper

2 large eggs

TO GARNISH

salad greens

tomato wedges

cucumber slices

dipping sauce, to serve

### COOK'S TIP

If you heat the skillet thoroughly
before adding the oil, and
heat the oil before adding
the ingredients, you should
not have a problem with
the ingredients sticking to
the skillet.

1 Heat half the oil in a large skillet. Add the garlic and cook over high heat for 30 seconds. Add the onion and the eggplant and continue to stir-fry until golden.

2 Add the bell pepper and stir-fry for an additional 1 minute to soften. Stir in the mushroom, tomato, soy sauce, sugar, and pepper. Remove from the skillet and keep hot.

3 Beat the eggs together lightly. Heat the remaining oil in a clean skillet, swirling to coat a wide area. Pour in the egg and swirl to set around the skillet.

4 When the egg is set, spoon the filling into the center. Fold in the sides of the omelet to form a square package.

5 Slide the omelet carefully on to a warmed dish and garnish with salad greens, tomato wedges, and cucumber slices. Serve with a dipping sauce.

# thai green salad

## serves four

1 small head romaine lettuce

1 bunch of scallions

½ cucumber

4 tbsp coarsely shredded and
toasted fresh coconut

DRESSING

4 tbsp lime juice

2 tbsp Thai fish sauce

1 small fresh red Thai chili,
finely chopped

1 tsp sugar

1 garlic clove, crushed

2 tbsp chopped cilantro

1 tbsp chopped fresh mint

### COOK'S TIP

This salad is good for picnics—to pack it easily, pack the leaves into a large plastic container or unbreakable salad bowl, and nestle the jar of dressing in the center. Cover with plastic wrap. Packed this way, the salad stays crisp, and if the dressing leaks during transit, there's no mess.

1 Tear or coarsely shred the lettuce leaves and place in a large salad bowl.

2 Trim and thinly slice the scallions diagonally, then add them to the salad bowl.

3 Use a vegetable peeler to shave thin slices along the length of the cucumber and add to the salad bowl.

4 Place all the ingredients for the dressing in a screw-top jar and shake well to mix thoroughly.

5 Pour the dressing over the salad and toss well to coat all the leaves evenly.

6 Sprinkle the coconut over the salad and toss in lightly just before serving.

# cucumber salad

## serves four

1 cucumber

1 tsp salt

1 small red onion

1 garlic clove, crushed

½ tsp chili paste

2 tsp Thai fish sauce

1 tbsp lime juice

1 tsp sesame oil

### COOK'S TIP

Once the salad is made, it can be chilled with the dressing for 1–2 hours, but is best eaten on the day of making.

### VARIATION

For a change, peel the cucumber and cut it into small dice shapes, then salt and drain as above. Drain and toss with the onions and dressing as before.

1 Trim the cucumber and coarsely grate the flesh. Place in a strainer over a large bowl, then sprinkle with the salt and let stand for 20 minutes. Discard the liquid.

2 Chop the onion finely, then toss into the cucumber. Spoon into 4 serving bowls. Alternatively, use a large serving dish.

3 Mix the garlic, chili paste, fish sauce, lime juice, and oil together in a small bowl, then spoon over the salad. Cover with plastic wrap and let chill in the refrigerator before serving.

# thai-style caesar salad

## serves four

1 large head romaine lettuce, with
   outer leaves removed, or 2 hearts
vegetable oil, for deep-frying
4–6 large rice paper wrappers or
   4 oz/115 g rice paper flakes
small bunch of cilantro, leaves
   stripped from stems
DRESSING
⅓ cup rice vinegar
2–3 tbsp Thai fish sauce
2 garlic cloves, coarsely chopped
1 tbsp sugar
1-inch/2.5-cm piece fresh
   gingerroot, coarsely chopped
½ cup corn oil
salt and pepper

1 Tear the lettuce leaves into bite-size pieces and place in a large salad bowl.

2 To make the dressing, place the vinegar, fish sauce, garlic, sugar, and ginger in a food processor and process for 15–30 seconds.

3 With the motor running, gradually pour in the corn oil until a creamy liquid forms. Season to taste with salt and pepper. Pour into a pitcher.

4 Heat 3 inches/7.5 cm of vegetable oil in a deep-fat fryer or wok to 350–375°F/180–190°C, or until a cube of bread browns in 30 seconds.

5 Meanwhile, break the rice wrappers into bite-size pieces and dip each into a bowl of water to soften. Lay on a clean dish towel and pat completely dry.

6 Working in batches, add the rice paper pieces to the hot oil and deep-fry for 15 seconds, or until crisp. Using a slotted spoon, transfer to paper towels to drain.

7 Add the cilantro leaves to the lettuce and toss to mix. Add the fried rice paper "chips" and drizzle over the dressing. Toss to coat the leaves and serve immediately.

### VARIATION
Substitute 2 tablespoons of the
corn oil with sesame oil for a
different flavor.

# green papaya salad

### serves four

8 oz/225 g snow peas

2 papayas

DRESSING

2 garlic cloves, crushed

2 fresh red chilies, seeded and
finely chopped

1 tsp sugar

2 tbsp soy sauce

juice of 1 lime

½ head Napa cabbage

TO GARNISH

12 cherry tomatoes

2 tbsp chopped peanuts

---

### VARIATION

Replace the chopped peanuts
with chopped cashew nuts, if
you prefer. For an extra touch,
lightly toast the nuts before
adding to the salad.

---

1 Place the snow peas in a pan of
boiling salted water. Return to a
boil and cook for 2 minutes. Drain
through a strainer, then refresh under
cold water. Cut into short thin sticks
and place in a bowl.

2 Peel the papayas, then remove
the black seeds and grate the
flesh into the bowl with the snow
peas. Cover and let chill in the
refrigerator until ready to serve.

3 Mix the garlic, chilies, sugar, soy
sauce, and lime juice together in
a bowl. Pour over the papaya salad
and mix well.

4 Arrange the Napa cabbage in a
large serving bowl, then place the
salad on top. Cut the cherry tomatoes
in half. Garnish the salad with
the tomatoes and chopped peanuts
before serving.

# pineapple & cucumber salad

## serves four

1 cucumber

1 small fresh pineapple

1 red onion, thinly sliced

1 bunch of watercress

DRESSING

3 tbsp lemon juice

2 tbsp soy sauce

1 tsp sugar

1 tsp chili sauce

2 tbsp chopped fresh mint

1 Peel the cucumber and cut into fourths lengthwise. Scoop out the seeds with a teaspoon and cut each quarter into ½-inch/1-cm pieces. Place in a bowl.

2 Peel the pineapple and cut into fourths lengthwise. Remove the core. Cut each fourth in half lengthwise, then cut into ½-inch/1-cm pieces and add to the cucumber. Add the onion and watercress and mix.

3 To make the dressing, place all ingredients in a small bowl and whisk together.

4 Pour the dressing over the salad and toss together. Transfer to a large serving platter and serve.

# thai salad with peanut dressing

## serves four

9 oz/250 g white cabbage,
   shredded

4 carrots, cut into short thin sticks

4 celery stalks, cut into short
   thin sticks

1⅔ cups fresh bean sprouts

½ cucumber, cut into short
   thin sticks

PEANUT SAUCE

2 tbsp smooth peanut butter

generous ¾ cups coconut cream

2 tsp Thai red curry paste

1 tbsp Thai fish sauce

1 tbsp brown sugar

TO GARNISH

fried onions

sliced fresh green chilli

3 To make the sauce, place all the ingredients in a pan. Heat gently, stirring, adding a little hot water, if necessary, to make a coating sauce.

4 Spoon a little of the sauce over the vegetables and garnish with fried onions and sliced chili. Serve the rest of the sauce separately.

1 Set a steamer above a pan of boiling water. Add the cabbage, carrots, and celery and steam for 3–4 minutes until just tender. Let cool.

2 Arrange the bean sprouts on a large, shallow serving dish. Arrange the cabbage, carrots, celery, and cucumber on top.

# grilled eggplant & sesame salad

## serves four

8 baby eggplants

salt

2 tsp chili oil

1 tbsp soy sauce

1 tbsp Thai fish sauce

1 tbsp corn oil

1 garlic clove, thinly sliced

1 fresh red Thai chili, seeded
  and sliced

1 tsp sesame oil

1 tbsp lime juice

1 tsp brown sugar

1 tbsp chopped fresh mint

1 tbsp sesame seeds, toasted

fresh mint leaves, to garnish

1 Cut the eggplants lengthwise into thin slices to within 1 inch/ 2.5 cm of the stem end. Place in a colander, sprinkling with salt between the slices, and let stand for 30 minutes. Rinse in cold water and pat dry with paper towels.

2 Preheat the broiler to medium. Mix the chili oil, soy sauce, and fish sauce together in a bowl, then brush over the eggplants. Cook under the hot broiler, or grill over hot coals,

for 6–8 minutes, turning them over occasionally and brushing with more chili oil glaze, until golden brown and softened. Arrange on a serving platter.

3 Heat the corn oil in a large skillet. Add the garlic and chili and cook for 1–2 minutes, until just beginning to brown. Remove the skillet from the heat and add the sesame oil, lime juice, sugar, and any remaining chili oil glaze.

4 Add the chopped mint and spoon the warm dressing over the eggplants. Let marinate for 20 minutes, then sprinkle with the toasted sesame seeds. Serve garnished with mint leaves.

# carrot & mango salad

## serves four

4 carrots

1 small ripe mango

7 oz/200 g firm tofu
   (drained weight)

1 tbsp snipped fresh chives

DRESSING

2 tbsp orange juice

1 tbsp lime juice

1 tsp clear honey

½ tsp orange flower water

1 tsp sesame oil

1 tsp sesame seeds, toasted

1 Coarsely grate the carrots. Peel, pit, and thinly slice the mango.

2 Cut the tofu into ½-inch/1-cm dice-shaped pieces and toss together with the carrots and mango in a wide salad bowl.

3 To make the dressing, place all the ingredients in a screw-top jar and shake well until thoroughly mixed. Pour the dressing over the salad and toss well to coat the salad evenly.

4 Just before serving, toss the salad lightly and sprinkle with snipped chives. Serve immediately.

**COOK'S TIP**

A food processor will grate the carrots in seconds—especially useful if you're catering for a crowd.

# thai seafood salad

## serves four

1 lb/450 g live mussels in shells

8 raw jumbo shrimp

12 oz/350 g squid, cleaned and
sliced widthwise into rings

4 oz/115 g cooked, shelled shrimp

1 red onion, finely sliced

1 red bell pepper, seeded and
finely sliced

⅔ cup fresh bean sprouts

4 oz/115 g shredded bok choy

DRESSING

1 garlic clove, crushed

1 tsp grated fresh gingerroot

1 fresh red chili, seeded and
finely chopped

2 tbsp chopped cilantro

1 tbsp lime juice

1 tsp finely grated lime rind

1 tbsp light soy sauce

5 tbsp corn or peanut oil

2 tsp sesame oil

salt and pepper

4 tbsp cold water

1 Clean the mussels by scrubbing or scraping the shells and pulling out any beards that are attached to them. Discard any with broken shells or any that refuse to close when tapped.

2 Place the mussels in a large pan with just the water that clings to their shells. Cook over high heat for 3–4 minutes, shaking the pan occasionally, until the mussels have opened. Discard any that remain closed. Strain the mussels, reserving the cooking liquid, and refresh under cold water. Drain again and reserve.

3 Bring the reserved cooking liquid to a boil and add the jumbo shrimp. Simmer for 5 minutes. Add the squid and cook for an additional 2 minutes, or until the shrimp and squid are cooked through. Remove with a slotted spoon and plunge into a bowl of cold water. Reserve the cooking liquid. Drain the shrimp and squid.

4 Remove the mussels from their shells and place in a bowl with the jumbo shrimp, squid, and cooked, shelled shrimp. Cover and let chill in the refrigerator for 1 hour.

5 To make the dressing, place all the ingredients, except the oils, in a food processor and process to a smooth paste. Add the oils, reserved cooking liquid, salt and pepper to taste, and water, then process again to mix.

6 Just before serving, mix the onion, bell pepper, bean sprouts, and bok choy in a bowl and toss with 2–3 tablespoons of the dressing. Arrange the vegetables on a large serving plate or in a bowl. Toss the remaining dressing with the seafood to coat and add to the vegetables. Serve immediately.

# thai noodle salad with shrimp

## serves four

3 oz/85 g rice vermicelli noodles or
  rice sticks

1⅔ cups snow peas, cut crosswise
  in half, if large

5 tbsp lime juice

4 tbsp Thai fish sauce

1 tbsp sugar, or to taste

1-inch/2.5-cm piece fresh
  gingerroot, finely chopped

1 fresh red chili, seeded and thinly
  sliced on the diagonal

4 tbsp chopped cilantro, plus extra
  for garnishing

4-inch/10-cm piece cucumber,
  peeled, seeded, and diced

2 scallions, thinly sliced
  on the diagonal

16–20 large cooked, shelled shrimp

2 tbsp chopped unsalted peanuts or
  cashews (optional)

TO GARNISH

4 cooked whole shrimp

lemon slices

### VARIATION

Replace the cilantro with the
same amount of mint and the
lemon slices with lime.

1 Place the rice noodles in a large
  bowl and pour over enough hot
water to cover. Let stand for 4 minutes,
or until soft. Drain and rinse under
cold running water, then drain again
and reserve.

2 Bring a pan of water to a boil.
  Add the snow peas and simmer
for 1 minute. Drain and rinse under
cold running water until cold, then
drain and reserve.

3 Whisk the lime juice, fish sauce,
  sugar, ginger, chili, and cilantro
together in a large bowl. Stir in the
cucumber and scallions. Add the
drained noodles, snow peas, and the
shrimp. Toss the salad gently together.

4 Divide the noodle salad between
  4 large plates. Sprinkle with
chopped cilantro and the peanuts,
if using, then garnish each plate with
a whole shrimp and a lemon slice.
Serve immediately.

### COOK'S TIP

There are many sizes of rice
noodles available—make sure
you use the thin rice noodles,
called rice vermicelli, rice sticks,
or *sen mee*, otherwise the salad
will be too heavy.

# broiled beef salad

1¾ oz/50 g dried oyster mushrooms

1 lb 5 oz/600 g rump steak

1 red bell pepper, seeded and
   thinly sliced

scant ⅓ cup roasted cashew nuts

red and green lettuce leaves

fresh mint leaves, to garnish

DRESSING

2 tbsp sesame oil

2 tbsp Thai fish sauce

2 tbsp sweet sherry

2 tbsp oyster sauce

1 tbsp lime juice

1 fresh red chili, seeded and
   finely chopped

1 Put the mushrooms in a heatproof
   bowl, cover with boiling water,
and let stand for 20 minutes. Drain,
then cut into slices.

2 Preheat the broiler to medium or
   heat a ridged grill pan. To make
the dressing, place all the ingredients
in a bowl and whisk to combine.

3 Cook the steak under the
   preheated grill or on the hot grill
pan, turning once, for 5 minutes, or
until browned on both sides but still
rare in the center. Cook the steak
longer if desired.

4 Slice the steak into thin strips
   and place in a bowl with the
mushrooms, bell pepper, and nuts.
Add the dressing and toss together.

5 Arrange the lettuce on a large
   serving platter and place the beef
mixture on top. Garnish with mint
leaves. Serve at room temperature.

# hot & sour beef salad

## serves four

1 tsp black peppercorns

1 tsp coriander seeds

1 red bird chili

¼ tsp Chinese five-spice powder

9 oz/250 g lean beef fillet

1 tbsp dark soy sauce

6 scallions

1 carrot

¼ cucumber

8 radishes

1 red onion

¼ head Napa cabbage

2 tbsp peanut oil

1 garlic clove, crushed

1 tsp finely chopped lemongrass

1 tbsp chopped fresh mint

1 tbsp chopped cilantro

DRESSING

3 tbsp lime juice

1 tbsp light soy sauce

2 tsp brown sugar

1 tsp sesame oil

1 Crush the peppercorns, coriander seeds, and chili in a mortar using a pestle, then mix with the five-spice powder and sprinkle on a plate. Brush the beef all over with soy sauce, then roll it in the spices to coat evenly.

2 Cut the scallions into 2½-inch/6-cm lengths, then shred them finely lengthwise. Place in a bowl of ice water and let stand until curled. Drain well.

3 Cut the carrot into very thin diagonal slices. Halve the cucumber lengthwise and scoop out the seeds, then slice thinly. Cut the radishes into flower shapes.

4 Slice the onion thinly, cutting each slice from top to root. Coarsely shred the Napa cabbage. Toss all the vegetables, except the scallion curls, together in a large salad bowl.

5 Heat the peanut oil in a large, heavy-bottom skillet. Add the garlic and lemongrass and cook until just turning golden brown. Add the beef and press down with a spatula to ensure it browns evenly. Cook for 3–4 minutes, turning it over once, depending on the thickness. Remove the skillet from the heat.

6 Slice the beef thinly and toss into the salad with the mint and cilantro. Mix all the ingredients for the dressing together in a bowl and stir into the skillet, then spoon over the salad. Garnish with the scallion curls and serve.

# roast duck salad

## serves four

2 duck breasts

2 Boston lettuces, shredded

¾ cup fresh bean sprouts

1 yellow bell pepper, seeded and
cut into thin strips

½ cucumber, seeded and cut
into short thin sticks

DRESSING

juice of 2 limes

3 tbsp Thai fish sauce

1 tbsp brown sugar

2 tsp sweet chili sauce

1-inch/2.5-cm piece fresh
gingerroot, finely grated

3 tbsp chopped fresh mint

3 tbsp chopped fresh basil

TO GARNISH

2 tsp shredded lime rind

2 tbsp shredded coconut, toasted

1 Preheat the oven to 400°F/200°C.
Place the duck breasts on a rack
set over a roasting pan and roast in the
oven for 20–30 minutes, or until
cooked as desired and the skin is crisp.
Remove from the oven and let cool.

2 Mix the lettuce, bean sprouts, bell
pepper, and cucumber together in
a large bowl. Cut the cooled duck into
strips and add to the salad. Mix well.

3 Whisk all the ingredients for the
dressing together in a separate
bowl. Add the dressing to the salad
and toss well.

4 Turn the salad out on to a serving
plate and garnish with lime rind
and shredded coconut before serving.

# Desserts & Drinks

The normal conclusion to a Thai meal is a basket of fruit, often including mangoes, mangosteens, jackfruit, guavas, and litchis. Desserts and sweetmeats are mostly made at home for between-meal treats, or made by experts for special occasions, because their preparation can be time-consuming and often requires skillful blending and shaping.

Rice, usually of the glutinous variety, and tapioca are vital ingredients in many candies and cakes, often molded or colored, soaked in scented syrups.

Many Thai drinks are colorful and exotic in flavor. They use the abundant fruits and coconut milk in long, refreshing drinks, sweetened with palm sugar and often served with a dash of whiskey or other spirit.

# thai rice pudding

## serves four

scant ½ cup short-grain rice

2 tbsp palm sugar

1 cardamom pod, split

1¼ cups coconut milk

⅔ cup water

3 eggs

generous ¾ cup coconut cream

1½ tbsp superfine sugar

sweetened coconut flakes,
    to decorate

fresh fruits, to serve

### COOK'S TIP

Cardamom is quite a powerful spice, so if you find it too strong, it can be left out or replaced with a little ground cinnamon.

1 Preheat the oven to 350°F/180°C. Place the rice and palm sugar in a pan. Remove the seeds from the cardamom pod and place in a mortar. Crush the seeds using a pestle, then add to the pan. Stir in the coconut milk and water.

2 Bring to a boil, stirring to dissolve the sugar. Reduce the heat and let simmer, uncovered, stirring occasionally, for 20 minutes, or until the rice is tender and most of the liquid is absorbed.

3 Spoon the rice into 4 individual ovenproof dishes and spread evenly. Place the dishes in a wide roasting pan and pour in enough water to come halfway up the sides.

4 Beat the eggs, coconut cream, and superfine sugar together in a bowl. Spoon over the rice. Cover with foil and bake in the preheated oven for 45–50 minutes, or until set.

5 Turn out the puddings and decorate with coconut flakes. Serve warm or cold with fresh fruit.

# strings of gold

## serves four

7 egg yolks

1 tbsp egg white

2½ cups granulated sugar

generous ¾ cup water

handful of fresh scented
   jasmine flowers

TO DECORATE

pomegranate seeds

sliced kiwifruit

sliced apple

1 Press the egg yolks and egg white through a fine strainer into a bowl, then whisk lightly.

2 Place the sugar and water in a large pan and heat gently until the sugar dissolves. Add the jasmine flowers, then bring to a boil and boil rapidly until a thin syrup forms. Remove the jasmine flowers with a slotted spoon and discard.

3 Bring the syrup to simmering point. Using a pastry bag with a fine nozzle, quickly drizzle the egg mixture into the syrup in a thin stream to form loose nests or pyramid shapes.

4 As soon as the threads set, remove the nests carefully and drain well on paper towels. Arrange in a warmed serving dish and decorate with the pomegranate seeds, kiwifruit, and apple. Serve immediately.

## VARIATION

If you can't get hold of fresh scented jasmine flowers, add a few drops of rose water or orange flower water to the syrup instead.

# mangoes in lemongrass syrup

## serves four

2 large ripe mangoes

1 lime

1 lemongrass stem, chopped

3 tbsp superfine sugar

### COOK'S TIP

To serve this dessert on a hot day, particularly if it is to stand for a while, place the dish on a bed of crushed ice to keep the fruits and syrup chilled.

1 Halve the mangoes, then remove the pits and peel off the skins.

2 Slice the flesh into long, thin slices and carefully arrange them in a wide serving dish.

3 Remove a few shreds of the rind from the lime for decoration, then cut the lime in half and squeeze out the juice.

4 Place the lime juice in a small pan with the lemongrass and sugar. Heat gently without boiling until the sugar is completely dissolved. Remove the pan from the heat and let cool completely.

5 Strain the cooled syrup into a small pitcher and pour evenly over the mango slices.

6 Sprinkle with the lime rind strips. Cover and let chill in the refrigerator before serving. Serve chilled.

# mango with sticky rice

## serves four

generous 1 cup glutinous rice, soaked
for 30 minutes in cold water

1 cup coconut milk

2 tbsp superfine sugar

pinch of salt

2 large ripe mangoes

1 Drain the rice and rinse
thoroughly. Place in a pan with
the coconut milk, sugar, and salt.
Bring to a boil and simmer, stirring
occasionally, until the rice has
absorbed all the coconut milk and is
very soft.

2 Transfer the rice to a steamer set
over a pan of simmering water.
Cover and steam for 15 minutes. Let
cool slightly. Press the rice into the
bottom of 4 ramekins and turn out on
to individual plates to form rice domes.
Alternatively, spread the rice out on a
baking sheet lined with foil, then roll
the rice flat with a wet rolling pin. Cut
into diamond shapes.

3 Peel the mangoes and cut the
flesh into cubes. Arrange the rice
diamonds and mango cubes on
individual plates or in ramekin dishes
and serve.

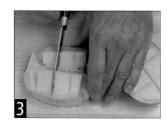

# exotic fruit salad

## serves six

1 tsp jasmine tea

1 tsp grated fresh gingerroot

juice of 1 lime plus 1 strip of
    lime rind

½ cup boiling water

2 tbsp superfine sugar

1 papaya

1 mango

½ small pineapple

1 carambola

2 passion fruit

### COOK'S TIP

Carambola have little flavor
when unripe and green, but once
ripened and yellow, they become
delicately sweet and fragrant.
Usually by this stage, the tips of
the ridges have become brown,
so you will need to remove these
before slicing. The easiest and
quickest method of doing this is
to run a vegetable peeler
along each ridge.

1 Place the tea, ginger, and lime rind in a heatproof pitcher and pour over the boiling water. Let infuse for 5 minutes, then strain the liquid.

2 Add the sugar to the liquid and stir well to dissolve. Let the syrup stand until it is completely cold.

3 Halve, seed, and peel the papaya. Halve the mango, then remove the pit and peel. Peel and remove the core from the pineapple. Cut the fruits into bite-size pieces.

4 Slice the carambola crosswise. Place the prepared fruits in a wide serving bowl and pour over the cooled syrup. Cover with plastic wrap and let chill in the refrigerator for 1 hour.

5 Cut the passion fruit in half, then scoop out the flesh with a teaspoon and mix with the lime juice. Spoon over the salad and serve.

# tropical fruit in lemongrass syrup

## serves four

1 honeydew melon

1 small pineapple

1 papaya

14 oz/400 g litchis, pitted

3 passion fruit

LEMONGRASS SYRUP

¾ cup superfine sugar

⅔ cup water

2 lemongrass stems, bruised

2 fresh kaffir lime leaves

juice of 1 lime

TO DECORATE

1 tbsp grated lime rind

small handful of fresh mint leaves

---

**VARIATION**

If fresh litchis are unavailable, replace them with drained canned ones.

---

1 To make the syrup, place all the ingredients in a pan. Heat gently until the sugar has dissolved. Bring to a boil and cook, uncovered, for 5 minutes. Let stand overnight.

2 Cut the melon in half, then remove the seeds and scoop out the flesh with a melon baller. Place in a bowl. Peel the pineapple, cut into fourths lengthwise, and remove the core. Cut into cubes and add to the melon. Peel the papaya, then remove the seeds, cut the flesh into cubes, and add to the other fruits.

3 Add the litchis. Cut the passion fruit in half and scoop the pulp and seeds into the bowl of fruits. Stir to mix, then transfer to a serving bowl. Remove the lemongrass and lime leaves from the syrup and pour over the fruits. Decorate with the lime rind and mint leaves and serve.

# mango & lime sherbet

## serves four

scant ½ cup superfine sugar

scant ½ cup water

finely grated rind of 3 limes

2 tbsp coconut cream

2 large ripe mangoes

scant ⅔ cup lime juice

curls of fresh coconut, toasted,
    to decorate

---

### VARIATION

If you prefer, canned mangoes in syrup can be used to make the sherbet. Omit the sugar and water, and infuse the lime rind in the canned syrup instead.

---

1 Place the sugar, water, and lime rind in a small pan and heat gently, stirring constantly, until the sugar dissolves. Boil rapidly for 2 minutes to reduce slightly, then remove the pan from the heat and strain into a heatproof bowl or pitcher. Stir in the coconut cream and let cool.

2 Halve the mangoes, then remove the pits and peel thinly. Chop the flesh coarsely and place in a food processor with the lime juice. Process to a smooth purée and transfer to a small bowl.

3 Pour the cooled syrup into the mango purée, mixing evenly. Tip into a large, freezerproof container and freeze for 1 hour, or until slushy in texture. Alternatively, use an ice cream machine.

4 Remove the container from the freezer and beat with an electric mixer to break up the ice crystals. Refreeze for an additional 1 hour, then remove from the freezer and beat the contents again until smooth.

5 Cover the container, then return to the freezer and leave until firm. To serve, remove from the freezer and let stand at room temperature for 15 minutes before scooping into individual glass dishes. Sprinkle with toasted coconut to decorate.

# rose ice

### serves four

1¾ cups water

2 tbsp coconut cream

4 tbsp sweetened condensed milk

2 tsp rose water

few drops of pink food
    coloring (optional)

pink rose petals, to decorate

1 Place the water in a small pan
and add the coconut cream.
Heat the mixture gently without
boiling, stirring.

2 Remove the pan from the heat
and let cool. Stir in the condensed
milk, rose water, and food coloring,
if using.

4 Remove the container from the
freezer and break up the ice
crystals with a fork. Return to the
freezer and freeze until firm.

3 Pour the mixture into a large,
freezerproof container and freeze
for 1–1½ hours, or until slushy.

5 Spoon the ice roughly into a pile
on a serving dish and sprinkle
with rose petals to decorate.

### COOK'S TIP
To prevent the ice thawing too
quickly at the table, nestle the
bottom of the serving dish in
another dish filled with
crushed ice.

# easy mango ice cream

### makes about 4 cups

2½ cups ready-made traditional custard

⅔ cup whipping cream, lightly whipped

flesh of 2 ripe mangoes, puréed

confectioners' sugar, to taste

passion fruit pulp, to serve

1 Mix the custard, cream, and mango purée together in a bowl.

2 Taste for sweetness and, if necessary, add confectioners' sugar to taste, remembering that when frozen, the mixture will taste less sweet.

3 Transfer the mixture to a large, freezerproof container. Cover and freeze for 2–3 hours, or until just frozen. Spoon into a bowl and mash with a fork or whisk to break down any ice crystals. Return the mixture to the container and freeze for an additional 2 hours. Mash once more, then freeze for 2–3 hours, or until firm.

4 Transfer the ice cream from the freezer to the refrigerator 20–30 minutes before serving. Serve with the passion fruit pulp.

# litchi & ginger sherbet

1 Drain the litchis, reserving the syrup. Place the litchis in a food processor or blender with the lime rind, juice, and preserved ginger syrup and process until completely smooth. Transfer to a large bowl.

**COOK'S TIP**

It is not recommended that raw eggs are served to very young children, pregnant women, the elderly, or anyone weakened by chronic illness. The egg whites may be left out of this recipe, but you will need to whisk the sherbet a second time after an additional 1 hour of freezing to obtain a light texture.

2 Mix the purée thoroughly with the reserved litchi syrup, then pour into a large, freezerproof container and freeze for 1–1½ hours, or until slushy in texture. Alternatively, use an ice cream machine.

3 Remove from the freezer and whisk to break up the ice crystals. Whisk the egg whites in a clean, dry bowl until stiff, then quickly and lightly fold into the ice mixture.

4 Return to the freezer and leave until firm. Serve the sherbet in scoops, with slices of carambola and preserved ginger to decorate.

# coconut & ginger ice cream

## makes about
## 4 cups

1¾ cups coconut milk

1 cup whipping cream

4 egg yolks

5 tbsp superfine sugar

4 tbsp preserved ginger syrup

6 pieces preserved ginger, finely
chopped

2 tbsp lime juice

fresh mint sprigs, to decorate

TO SERVE

litchis

preserved ginger syrup

1 Place the coconut milk and cream in a pan. Heat gently until just beginning to simmer. Remove the pan from the heat.

2 Beat the egg yolks, sugar, and ginger syrup together in a large bowl until pale and creamy. Slowly pour in the hot coconut milk mixture, stirring. Return to the pan and heat gently, stirring constantly, until the mixture thickens and coats the back of a spoon. Remove the pan from the heat and let cool. Stir in the ginger and lime juice.

3 Transfer the mixture to a large, freezerproof container. Cover and freeze for 2–3 hours, or until just frozen. Spoon into a bowl and mash with a fork or whisk to break down any ice crystals. Return the mixture to the container and freeze for an additional 2 hours. Mash once more, then freeze for 2–3 hours, or until firm.

4 Transfer to the refrigerator 20–30 minutes before serving. Decorate with mint sprigs and serve with litchis and a little ginger syrup drizzled over.

# pineapple with cardamom & lime

1 pineapple

2 cardamom pods

thinly pared lime rind

4 tbsp water

1 tbsp brown sugar

3 tbsp lime juice

TO DECORATE

fresh mint sprigs

whipped cream

---

### COOK'S TIP

To remove the "eyes" from pineapple, cut off the peel, then use a small, sharp knife to cut a V-shaped channel down the pineapple, cutting diagonally through the lines of brown "eyes" in the flesh, to make spiraling cuts around the fruit.

---

1 Cut the top and base from the pineapple, then cut away the peel and remove the "eyes" from the flesh (see Cook's Tip). Cut into fourths and remove the core. Slice the pineapple lengthwise and place in a large serving dish.

2 Crush the cardamom pods in a mortar using a pestle and place in a pan with the lime rind and water. Bring the mixture to a boil, then reduce the heat and simmer for 30 seconds.

3 Remove the pan from the heat and add the sugar, then cover with a lid and let infuse for 5 minutes.

4 Stir in the sugar to dissolve, add the lime juice, then strain the syrup over the pineapple. Cover and let chill in the refrigerator for 30 minutes.

5 When ready to serve, decorate with mint sprigs and a spoonful of whipped cream.

# mung bean custards

## serves six

4½ oz/125 g dried mung beans

2 eggs, beaten

¾ cup coconut milk

½ cup superfine sugar

1 tbsp ground rice

1 tsp ground cinnamon, plus extra
   for sprinkling

butter, for greasing

TO DECORATE

sour cream or whipped cream

finely grated lime rind

sliced carambola

pomegranate seeds

1 Preheat the oven to 350°F/180°C.
Place the dried mung beans in a
pan with enough water to cover. Bring
to a boil, then reduce the heat and
simmer for 30–40 minutes, or until the
beans are very tender. Drain well.

### COOK'S TIP

To save time, use canned mung
beans. Drain the beans
thoroughly, then mash and purée
them and add to the bowl with
the eggs and coconut milk.

2 Mash the beans, then press
through a strainer to form a
smooth purée. Place the bean purée,
eggs, coconut milk, sugar, ground rice,
and cinnamon in a large bowl and
beat well until mixed.

3 Grease and line the bottom of
4 x ⅔-cup pudding-shaped molds
or ramekin dishes and pour in the
mixture. Place on a baking sheet in
the preheated oven and bake for
20–25 minutes, or until just set.

4 Let the custards cool in the molds,
then run a knife around the edges
to loosen and turn out on to individual
serving plates. Sprinkle with cinnamon.
Decorate with sour cream, lime rind,
carambola, and pomegranate seeds.

# balinese banana crêpes

scant 1½ cups all-purpose flour

pinch of salt

4 eggs, beaten

2 large ripe bananas, mashed

1¼ cups coconut milk

vegetable oil, for frying

TO DECORATE

sliced bananas

6 tbsp lime juice

confectioners' sugar

coconut cream, to serve

1 Place the flour, salt, eggs, bananas, and coconut milk in a food processor or blender and process to a smooth batter. Alternatively, sift the flour and salt into a bowl and make a well in the center, then add the remaining ingredients and beat well until smooth.

2 Let the batter chill in the refrigerator for 1 hour. Remove the batter from the refrigerator and beat briefly again. Heat a small amount of oil in a small skillet until very hot.

3 Drop tablespoonfuls of the batter into the skillet. Cook until the crêpes are golden underneath.

4 Turn over and cook the other sides until golden brown. Cook in batches until all the batter is used up, making 36 crêpes. Remove and let drain on paper towels.

5 Arrange the crêpes in a stack, layered with sliced bananas, sprinkled with lime juice and sugar. Serve with coconut cream.

# caramel apple wedges with sesame seeds

## serves four

1 cup rice flour

1 egg

½ cup cold water

4 crisp dessert apples

2½ tbsp sesame seeds

1¼ cups superfine sugar

2 tbsp vegetable oil, plus extra for
   deep-frying

fresh basil sprigs, to decorate

1 Place the flour, egg, and water in a large bowl and whisk well until a smooth, thick batter forms.

2 Core the apples and cut each into 8 wedges. Drop into the batter and stir in the sesame seeds.

3 Place the sugar and the 2 tablespoons of oil in a heavy-bottom skillet and heat, stirring, until the sugar dissolves. Continue until the syrup begins to turn golden. Remove the skillet from the heat but keep warm.

### COOK'S TIP

Take care not to overheat the sugar syrup, otherwise it will become difficult to handle and burn. If it begins to set before you have finished dipping the apple pieces, warm it slightly until it becomes liquid again.

4 Heat the oil for deep-frying in a deep skillet or wok to 350–375°F/180–190°C, or until a cube of bread browns in 30 seconds. Lift the apple pieces one by one from the batter using tongs, lower into the hot oil, and deep-fry for 2–3 minutes, or until golden brown and crisp.

5 Remove with a slotted spoon and dip very quickly into the sugar mixture. Dip the apple wedges briefly into a bowl of ice water and drain on paper towels. Transfer to a serving plate, then decorate with basil and serve immediately.

# banana fritters in coconut batter

## serves four

½ cup all-purpose flour

2 tbsp rice flour

1 tbsp superfine sugar

1 egg, separated

⅔ cup coconut milk

corn oil, for deep-frying

4 large bananas

TO DECORATE

1 tsp confectioners' sugar

1 tsp ground cinnamon

lime wedges

### COOK'S TIP

If you can buy the baby finger bananas that are popular in this dish in the East, leave them whole for coating and frying.

1 Sift the all-purpose flour, rice flour, and sugar into a bowl and make a well in the center. Add the egg yolk and coconut milk.

2 Beat the mixture until a smooth, thick batter forms. Whisk the egg white in a clean, dry bowl until stiff, then fold it into the batter lightly and evenly.

3 Heat a 2½-inch/6-cm depth of oil in a large skillet to 350–375°F/180–190°C, or until a cube of bread browns in 30 seconds. Cut the bananas in half crosswise, then dip them quickly into the batter to coat them.

4 Drop the bananas carefully into the hot oil and cook in batches for 2–3 minutes, or until golden brown, turning once.

5 Drain on paper towels. Sprinkle with sugar and cinnamon and decorate with lime wedges.

# coconut crêpes

1 cup rice flour

scant ¼ cup superfine sugar

pinch of salt

2 eggs

2½ cups coconut milk

4 tbsp dry unsweetened coconut

vegetable oil, for frying

2 tbsp palm sugar, for sprinkling

fresh mango or banana, to serve

1 Place the rice flour, superfine sugar, and salt in a bowl and add the eggs and coconut milk, whisking until a smooth batter forms. Alternatively, place all the ingredients in a food processor or blender and process to a smooth batter. Beat in half the coconut.

2 Heat a small amount of oil in a wide, heavy-bottom skillet. Pour in a little batter, swirling the skillet to cover the surface thinly and evenly. Cook until the crêpe is pale golden underneath.

3 Turn the crêpe and cook quickly to brown lightly on the other side.

4 Remove the crêpe from the skillet and keep hot while using the remaining batter to make a total of 8 crêpes.

5 Lightly toast the remaining coconut and reserve. Transfer the crêpes folded or loosely rolled to serving plates. Sprinkle with palm sugar and the toasted coconut and serve with slices of mango or banana.

# crêpes with papaya & passion fruit

## serves four

2 eggs

½ cup coconut milk

¾ cup milk

generous ¾ cup all-purpose flour

pinch of salt

1 tbsp superfine sugar

1 tbsp butter, melted

vegetable oil, for frying

sifted confectioners' sugar, for dusting

FILLING

2 papayas

3 passion fruit

juice of 1 lime

2 tbsp confectioners' sugar

### COOK'S TIP

To enjoy these crêpes at their very best, serve this dessert as soon as it has been assembled.

1 Whisk the eggs, coconut milk, and milk together in a bowl. Sift the flour and salt into a separate bowl. Stir in the superfine sugar. Make a well in the center of the flour and gradually beat in the egg mixture to form a smooth batter. Stir in the melted butter.

2 Heat an 8–9-inch/20–23-cm nonstick skillet and brush with oil. Pour in enough batter to coat the bottom. Tip the skillet as you pour it in, so the bottom is evenly coated. Cook until browned on the underside and set on top, then turn the crêpe over and cook the other side. Place on a plate, cover with foil, and keep warm while making the remaining crêpes.

3 Peel the papayas, then cut in half and scoop out the seeds, reserving a few. Cut into chunks and place in a bowl. Cut the passion fruit in half and scoop the seeds and pulp into the bowl. Stir in the lime juice and confectioners' sugar. Put a little filling on one-fourth of each crêpe. Fold in half and then into fourths. Dust with sifted confectioners' sugar. Sprinkle the reserved papaya seeds over and serve at once.

# coconut custard squares

## serves four

1 tsp butter, melted

6 eggs

1¾ cups coconut milk

scant 1 cup brown sugar

pinch of salt

TO DECORATE

shreds of coconut

strips of lime rind

fresh fruit slices, to serve

### COOK'S TIP

Keep an eye on the custard as it bakes, because if it overcooks, the texture will be spoiled. When the custard comes out of the oven, it should be barely set and still slightly wobbly in the center. It will firm up slightly as it cools.

**1** Preheat the oven to 350°F/180°C. Brush the melted butter over the inside of a 7½-inch/19-cm square ovenproof dish, about 1½ inches/ 4 cm in depth.

**2** Beat the eggs in a large bowl, then beat in the coconut milk, sugar, and salt.

**3** Place the bowl over a pan of gently simmering water and stir with a wooden spoon for 15 minutes, or until it begins to thicken. Pour into the prepared dish.

**4** Bake in the preheated oven for 20–25 minutes, or until just set. Remove the dish from the oven and let cool completely.

**5** Turn the custard out of the dish and cut into squares. Serve decorated with coconut shreds and lime rind together with slices of fruit.

# bananas in coconut milk

## serves four

4 large bananas

1½ cups coconut milk

2 tbsp superfine sugar

pinch of salt

1 tsp orange flower water

1 tbsp shredded fresh mint

2 tbsp cooked mung beans

fresh mint sprigs, to decorate

1 Peel the bananas and cut them into short chunks. Place in a large pan with the coconut milk, sugar, and salt.

2 Heat gently until boiling and simmer for 1 minute. Remove the pan from the heat.

3 Sprinkle the orange flower water over the banana mixture. Stir in the mint and spoon into a serving dish.

4 Place the mung beans in a heavy-bottom skillet and cook over high heat until they turn crisp and golden, shaking the skillet occasionally. Let the beans cool slightly, then crush lightly in a mortar using a pestle.

5 Sprinkle the toasted beans over the bananas and serve warm or cold, decorated with mint sprigs.

# sticky rice shapes

## serves four

scant 1½ cups glutinous rice

2½ cups granulated sugar

1¼ cups water

few drops of rose water or
   jasmine extract

pink and green food colorings

rose petals or jasmine flowers,
   to decorate

1 Place the rice in a bowl and add
   enough cold water to cover. Let
soak for 3 hours or overnight.

2 Drain the rice and rinse
   thoroughly in cold water. Line the
top part of a steamer with cheesecloth
and tip the rice into it. Place over
boiling water, then cover and steam for
30 minutes. Remove the rice from the
steamer and let cool.

3 Heat the sugar and water gently
   in a pan until the sugar dissolves.
Add the rose water. Bring to a boil and
boil for 4–5 minutes to reduce to a thin
syrup. Remove the pan from the heat.

4 Divide the rice in half and color
   one half pale pink, the other half
pale green. Form into small balls or
shapes using molds (see Cook's Tip).

5 Using 2 forks, dip the rice shapes
   into the syrup. Drain off the
excess syrup and pile on to a dish.
Decorate with rose petals or jasmine
flowers and serve.

### COOK'S TIP

If you prefer, the rice can be
shaped in small sweet molds or
dariole molds to produce small
castle or turret shapes.

# coconut cake with lime & ginger syrup

## serves four

2 large eggs, separated

pinch of salt

½ cup superfine sugar

5 tbsp butter, melted and
cooled

5 tbsp coconut milk

1 cup self-rising flour

½ tsp baking powder

3 tbsp dry unsweetened coconut

4 tbsp preserved ginger syrup

3 tbsp lime juice

TO DECORATE

3 pieces preserved ginger

curls of fresh coconut

finely grated lime rind

1 Cut an 11-inch/28-cm circle of parchment paper and press into a 7-inch/18-cm steamer basket to line it.

2 Whisk the egg whites with the salt in a clean, dry bowl until stiff. Gradually whisk in the sugar, 1 tablespoon at a time, whisking hard after each addition until the mixture forms stiff peaks.

3 Whisk in the yolks, then quickly stir in the butter and coconut milk. Sift the flour and baking powder over the mixture, then fold in lightly and evenly with a large metal spoon. Fold in the coconut.

4 Spoon the mixture into the lined steamer basket and tuck the spare paper over the top. Place the basket over boiling water, then cover and steam for 30 minutes.

5 Transfer the cake to a plate, remove the paper, and let cool slightly. Mix the ginger syrup and lime juice together and spoon over the cake. Cut into squares and decorate with pieces of preserved ginger, curls of coconut, and lime rind.

# melon & ginger crush

## serves four

1 melon, about 1 lb 12 oz/800 g

6 tbsp ginger wine

3 tbsp kaffir lime juice or lime juice

crushed ice

1 lime

1 Peel, seed, and coarsely chop the melon. Place the melon in a food processor or blender with the ginger wine and lime juice.

2 Blend together on high speed until the melon mixture is smooth.

3 Place plenty of crushed ice in 4 tall glasses. Pour the melon and ginger crush over the ice.

4 Cut the lime into thin slices, then cut a slit in 4 of the slices and slip one on to the side of each glass. Add the remaining slices of lime to each glass, then serve immediately.

### VARIATION

If you prefer a nonalcoholic version of this drink, simply omit the ginger wine, then top up with ginger ale in the glass. For a change of flavor, use a watermelon when they are in season. Ginger wine is available from specialty wine merchants.

# tropical fruit punch

## serves six

1 small ripe mango

4 tbsp lime juice

1 tsp finely grated fresh gingerroot

1 tbsp brown sugar

1¼ cups orange juice

1¼ cups pineapple juice

1¼ cups rum

crushed ice

TO DECORATE

orange slices

lime slices

pineapple slices

carambola slices

1 Peel and pit the mango and chop the flesh. Place in a food processor or blender with the lime juice, ginger, and sugar and process until smooth.

2 Add the orange and pineapple juices, then add the rum and process again for a few seconds until blended. Divide the crushed ice between 6 glasses and pour the punch over the ice.

3 Add orange and lime slices, then arrange the pineapple and carambola slices on the rim of each glass. Serve immediately.

# lime & lemongrass cooler

## serves four

egg white

3 tbsp superfine sugar, plus extra
    for frosting

2 limes

1 small lemongrass stem

4 ice cubes

½ cup water

4 lime slices

soda water

1 To frost the rims of the glasses,
pour a little egg white into a
saucer. Spread a small amount of sugar
out on a plate. Dip the rim of each
glass briefly into the egg white, then
into the sugar.

2 Cut each lime into 8 pieces and
coarsely chop the lemongrass.
Place the lime pieces and lemongrass
in a food processor or blender with the
sugar and ice cubes.

3 Add the water and process for a
few seconds. Try not to
overprocess, otherwise the drink will
have a bitter flavor.

4 Strain the mixture into the frosted
glasses. Add a lime slice to each
glass and top up with soda water to
taste. Serve immediately.

# mango & coconut smoothie

## serves four

2 large ripe mangoes

1 tbsp confectioners' sugar

generous 2 cups coconut milk

5 ice cubes

slivered, toasted coconut, to serve

### COOK'S TIP

To add a special kick to this drink, add a generous dash of white rum to the food processor or blender with the coconut milk.

1 Using a sharp knife, cut the mangoes in half and remove the pit. Peel and coarsely chop the flesh.

2 Place the chopped flesh in a food processor or blender with the sugar and process until completely smooth.

3 Add the coconut milk and ice cubes to the food processor or blender and process until frothy.

4 Pour into 4 tall glasses and sprinkle with slivered, toasted coconut to serve.

### VARIATION

If you don't have slivered, toasted coconut, sprinkle with ground ginger, cinnamon, or nutmeg just before serving.

# thai cocktail sling

## serves one

2 tbsp whiskey

1 tbsp cherry brandy

1 tbsp orange-flavored liqueur

1 tbsp lime juice

1 tsp palm sugar

dash of Angostura bitters

2 ice cubes

½ cup pineapple juice

1 small pineapple wedge

1 Place the whiskey, cherry brandy, liqueur, lime juice, sugar, and Angostura bitters in a cocktail shaker. Shake well to mix thoroughly.

2 Place the ice cubes in a large glass. Pour the cocktail mixture over the ice, then top up with the pineapple juice.

3 Cut a slit in the pineapple wedge and arrange on the edge of the glass. Serve immediately.

### COOK'S TIP

If the pineapple juice is quite sweet, as Thai pineapple juice is, you may not need to add sugar. So if you're unsure, taste first. Scotch whisky is very highly regarded in Thailand, although a powerful whiskey is distilled locally—if you have the stomach for it!

## A

apple
  caramel apple wedges with sesame seeds 237
avocado
  chilled avocado, lime & cilantro soup 22

## B

bamboo shoot salad 192
banana leaves
  chicken fried in banana leaves 53
  salmon with red curry in banana leaves 80
  steamed crab cakes 38
bananas
  Balinese banana crêpes 236
  banana fritters in coconut batter 238
  bananas in coconut milk 243
basil 6
  baked fish with bell pepper, chilies & basil 68
  egg noodle salad with lime & basil dressing 157
  jasmine rice with lemon & basil 156
  steamed mussels with lemongrass & basil 42
  stir-fried chicken with Thai basil 122
beef
  beef & bell peppers with lemongrass 90
  beef & coconut curry 91, 98
  beef satay with peanut sauce 96
  broiled beef salad 210
  hot & sour beef salad 212
  hot beef & coconut curry 98
  red-hot beef with cashew nuts 94
  stir-fried beef with bean sprouts 92
bell peppers
  baked fish with bell pepper, chilies & basil 68
  beef & bell peppers with lemongrass 90
  noodles with shrimp & green bell peppers 139
  roasted spiced bell peppers 173
bok choy with crabmeat 191
burgers 109

## C

caesar salad 199
carrot & mango salad 205
cashew nuts
  red-hot beef with cashew nuts 94
  spiced cashew nut curry 168
chicken
  aromatic chicken & vegetable soup 21
  braised chicken with garlic & spices 128
  chicken & coconut milk soup 18
  chicken & mango stir-fry 120
  chicken balls with dipping sauce 54
  chicken fried in banana leaves 53
  chicken noodle soup 16
  chicken satay 50
  chicken with lemongrass & chili 123
  crispy rice noodles 136
  drunken noodles 146
  green chicken curry 118, 126
  lemongrass chicken skewers 46
  peanut-crusted chicken 130

  quick green chicken curry 126
  red chicken with cherry tomatoes 117
  rice noodles with chicken & Napa cabbage 144
  roast chicken with ginger & lime 116
  shrimp & chicken sesame toasts 33
  spiced cilantro chicken 124
  sticky ginger chicken wings 52
  stir-fried chicken with Thai basil 122
  stuffed chicken wings 48
chilies 5, 6
  baked fish with pepper, chilies & basil 68
  chicken with lemongrass & chili 123
  chili & coconut sambal 176
  chili-spiced shrimp won ton soup 10
  crispy tofu with chili-soy sauce 186
  duck breasts with chili & lime 131
  hot chili relish with crudités 51
  spicy scallops with lime & chili 86
  vegetable fritters with sweet chili dip 188
cilantro 6
  chilled avocado, lime & cilantro soup 22
  sesame noodles with shrimp & cilantro 140
  spiced cilantro chicken 124
clams
  spicy Thai seafood stew 75
coconut 5
  chili & coconut sambal 176
  coconut cake with lime & ginger syrup 246
  coconut crêpes 239
  coconut rice with pineapple 158
  coconut shrimp 81
  potatoes in creamed coconut 178
  pumpkin & coconut soup 25
  Thai-style noodle röstis 148
  vegetable & coconut curry 182
coconut milk 6
  banana fritters in coconut batter 238
  bananas in coconut milk 243
  beef & coconut curry 91, 98
  chicken & coconut milk soup 18
  coconut & ginger ice cream 231
  coconut crêpes 239
  coconut custard squares 242
  coconut rice with pineapple 158
  green chicken curry 118
  mango & coconut smoothie 251
  mango with sticky rice 222
  mung bean custards 234
  roasted duckling with pineapple & coconut 132
corn
  corn fritters 190
  creamy corn soup with egg 24
  spicy fried rice 154
  stir-fried pork & corn 104
crab
  bok choy with crabmeat 191
  crab omelet 37
  creamy corn soup with egg 24
  open crabmeat sandwiches 36
  potato crab cakes 39

  steamed crab cakes 38
  stuffed eggs with pork & crabmeat 56
creamed coconut see coconut
crêpes
  Balinese banana crêpes 236
  coconut crêpes 239
  crêpes with papaya & passion fruit 240
cucumber salad 198
  pineapple & cucumber salad 202
curry
  baked cod with a curry crust 74
  beef & coconut curry 91, 98
  curried mussel soup 70
  fish curry 67
  green chicken curry 118, 126
  hot beef & coconut curry 98
  potato & spinach yellow curry 179
  quick green chicken curry 126
  red bean curry 180
  red lamb curry 112
  salmon with red curry in banana leaves 80
  shrimp & pineapple curry 87
  spiced cashew nut curry 168
  vegetable & coconut curry 182
curry paste 7

## D

desserts 218–247
dipping sauce 54
drinks 248–253
duck
  crispy duck with noodles & tamarind 152
  duck breasts with chili & lime 131
  roast duck salad 214
  roasted duckling with pineapple & coconut 132

## E

egg noodles see noodles
eggplant
  broiled eggplant & sesame salad 204
  eggplant & mushroom stuffed omelet 195
eggs
  creamy corn soup with egg 24
  fried egg noodles 143
  rice soup with eggs 11
  stir-fried rice with egg strips 160
  strings of gold 220
  stuffed eggs with pork & crabmeat 56
  see also omelets; crêpes

## F

fish
  baked cod with a curry crust 74
  baked fish with bell pepper, chilies & basil 68
  fish cakes with hot peanut dip 32
  fish cakes with sweet & sour dip 71
  fish curry 67
  pan-fried spiced salmon 78
  rice with seafood 162
  salmon with red curry in banana leaves 80

spiced steamed fish 76
spiced tuna in sweet & sour sauce 79
spicy Thai seafood stew 75
steamed yellow fish fillets 66
tuna & tomato salad with ginger dressing 60
whole fried fish with soy & ginger 72
*see also* seafood
fish sauce 7
fritters
  banana fritters in coconut batter 238
  corn fritters 190
  vegetable fritters with sweet chili dip 188
fruit salad 223

**G**
galangal 7
garlic 7
  braised chicken with garlic & spices 128
ginger 7
  coconut & ginger ice cream 231
  coconut cake with lime & ginger syrup 246
  litchi & ginger sherbet 230
  melon & ginger crush 248
  roast chicken with ginger & lime 116
  spinach & ginger soup 26
  sticky ginger chicken wings 52
  stir-fried ginger mushrooms 170
  tuna & tomato salad with ginger dressing 60
  whole fried fish with soy & ginger 72
green chicken curry 118, 126
green salad 196
  green papaya salad 200

**H**
hot & sour
  beef salad 212
  noodle salad 142
  noodles 145
  soup 15

**I, J, K**
ice cream
  coconut & ginger ice cream 231
  easy mango ice cream 229
  rose ice 228
  *see also* sherbet
jumbo shrimp *see* shrimp
kaffir lime leaves 7
  lamb with lime leaves 110

**L**
lamb
  lamb with lime leaves 110
  red lamb curry 112
  stir-fried lamb with mint 114
lemongrass 7
  beef & bell peppers with lemongrass 90
  chicken with lemongrass & chili 123
  lemongrass chicken skewers 46
  lime & lemongrass cooler 250

mangoes in lemongrass syrup 221
pork steaks with lemongrass 103
steamed mussels with lemongrass & basil 42
tropical fruit in lemongrass syrup 224
lettuce
  asian lettuce cups 194
  pork appetizer in lettuce cups 57
lime
  chilled avocado, lime & cilantro soup 22
  coconut cake with lime & ginger syrup 246
  duck breasts with chili & lime 131
  egg noodle salad with lime & basil dressing 157
  kaffir lime leaves 7
  lamb with lime leaves 110
  lime & lemongrass cooler 250
  mango & lime sherbet 226
  pineapple with cardamom & lime 232
  roast chicken with ginger & lime 116
  spicy scallops with lime & chili 86

**M**
mango
  carrot & mango salad 205
  chicken & mango stir-fry 120
  easy mango ice cream 229
  mango & coconut smoothie 251
  mango & lime sherbet 226
  mango with sticky rice 222
  mangoes in lemongrass syrup 221
  tropical fruit punch 249
meat *see* beef; chicken; duck; lamb; pork; turkey
melon & ginger crush 248
mung bean custards 234
mushrooms
  broiled beef salad 210
  eggplant & mushroom stuffed omelet 195
  hot & sour noodles 145
  mushroom & tofu broth 20
  rice noodles with mushrooms & tofu 138
  spiced mushrooms 172
  spicy fried rice 154
  stir-fried ginger mushrooms 170
  tom yam gung 12
mussels
  curried mussel soup 70
  fragrant mussels 41
  mussels in spiced batter 40
  rice with seafood 162
  steamed mussels with lemongrass & basil 42
  sweet & sour seafood salad 62
  Thai seafood salad 206

**N**
nam pla (fish sauce) 7
noodles
  chicken noodle soup 16
  crispy duck with noodles & tamarind 152
  crispy rice noodles 136
  drunken noodles 146
  egg noodle salad with lime & basil dressing 157

fried egg noodles 143
hot & sour noodle salad 142
hot & sour noodles 145
noodles with shrimp & green bell peppers 139
pad thai noodles 147
rice noodles with chicken & Napa cabbage 144
rice noodles with mushrooms & tofu 138
rice noodles with spinach 150
sesame noodles with shrimp & cilantro 140
Thai noodle salad with shrimp 208
Thai-style noodle röstis 148
nuts *see* cashew nuts; peanuts

**O**
omelets
  crab omelet 37
  eggplant & mushroom stuffed omelet 195
  pork-stuffed omelet 58

**P**
pad thai noodles 147
palm sugar 7
papaya
  crêpes with papaya & passion fruit 240
  green papaya salad 200
peanuts
  beef satay with peanut sauce 96
  crispy pork & peanut baskets 45
  fish cakes with hot peanut dip 32
  mixed vegetables in peanut sauce 169
  peanut-crusted chicken 130
  Thai salad with peanut dressing 203
pineapple
  coconut rice with pineapple 158
  pineapple & cucumber salad 202
  pineapple with cardamom & lime 232
  roasted duckling with pineapple & coconut 132
  shrimp & pineapple curry 87
pork
  crispy pork & peanut baskets 45
  drunken noodles 146
  pad thai noodles 147
  pork appetizer in lettuce cups 57
  pork steaks with lemongrass 103
  pork-stuffed omelet 58
  pork with soy & sesame glaze 105
  rice soup with eggs 11
  roasted red pork 102
  roasted spare ribs with honey & soy 44
  spiced pork sausages 108
  spicy fried ground pork 100
  spring rolls 55
  steamed won ton bundles 47
  stir-fried pork & corn 104
  stuffed chicken wings 48
  stuffed eggs with pork & crabmeat 56
  tamarind pork 106
  Thai-style burgers 109
potatoes
  potato & spinach yellow curry 179

potato crab cakes 39
potatoes in creamed coconut 178
sweet & sour potato stir-fry 177
sweet potato cakes with soy-tomato sauce 174
poultry see chicken; duck; turkey
pumpkin & coconut soup 25
punch 249

**R**
red curry
red bean curry 180
red chicken with cherry tomatoes 117
red lamb curry 112
salmon with red curry in banana leaves 80
rice 5
coconut rice with pineapple 158
jasmine rice with lemon & basil 156
mango with sticky rice 222
rice soup with eggs 11
rice with seafood 162
spicy fried rice 154
sticky rice shapes 244
stir-fried rice with egg strips 160
Thai rice pudding 218
rice noodles see noodles
rice vinegar 7
rose ice 228

**S**
salads 60, 62, 142, 192–215
salmon
pan-fried spiced salmon 78
salmon with red curry in banana leaves 80
satay
beef satay with peanut sauce 96
chicken satay 50
scallops
spicy scallops with lime & chili 86
sweet & sour seafood salad 62
Thai seafood soup 14
seafood
rice with seafood 162
soup 14
sweet & sour seafood salad 62
Thai seafood salad 206
see also clams; crab; fish; mussels; scallops;
shrimp; squid
sesame
broiled eggplant & sesame salad 204
caramel apple wedges with sesame seeds 237
pork with soy & sesame glaze 105
sesame noodles with shrimp & cilantro 140
shrimp & chicken sesame toasts 33
sherbet
litchi & ginger sherbet 230
mango & lime sherbet 226
see also ice cream
shrimp
chili-spiced shrimp won ton soup 10
coconut shrimp 81

hot & sour soup 15
jumbo shrimp rolls with sweet soy sauce 30
jumbo shrimp skewers 34
noodles with shrimp & green bell peppers 139
pad thai noodles 147
rice noodles with spinach 150
rice with seafood 162
sesame noodles with shrimp & cilantro 140
shrimp & chicken sesame toasts 33
shrimp & pineapple curry 87
shrimp skewers with tamarind glaze 82
spicy fried rice 154
spicy Thai seafood stew 75
spicy Thai soup with shrimp 19
spring rolls 55
stuffed chicken wings 48
sweet & sour seafood salad 62
Thai noodle salad with shrimp 208
Thai seafood salad 206
Thai seafood soup 14
tom yam gung 12
soups 9–27
soy sauce 7
crispy tofu with chili-soy sauce 186
jumbo shrimp rolls with sweet soy sauce 30
pork with soy & sesame glaze 105
roasted spare ribs with honey & soy 44
sweet potato cakes with soy-tomato sauce 174
whole fried fish with soy & ginger 72
spare ribs
roasted with honey & soy 44
spinach
potato & spinach yellow curry 179
rice noodles with spinach 150
spinach & ginger soup 26
spring rolls 55
vegetarian 59
squid
rice with seafood 162
spicy Thai seafood stew 75
stir-fried squid with hot black bean sauce 84
sweet & sour seafood salad 62
Thai seafood salad 206
stew
spicy Thai seafood stew 75
stir-fry
beef with bean sprouts 92
broccoli in oyster sauce 187
chicken & mango 120
chicken with Thai basil 122
ginger mushrooms 170
green vegetables 167
lamb with mint 114
pork & corn 104
rice with egg strips 160
squid with hot black bean sauce 84
sweet & sour potato 177
strings of gold 220
sweet & sour
fish cakes with sweet & sour dip 71

spiced tuna in sweet & sour sauce 79
sweet & sour potato stir-fry 177
sweet & sour seafood salad 62

**T**
tamarind paste 7
crispy duck with noodles & tamarind 152
shrimp skewers with tamarind glaze 82
tamarind pork 106
tofu
carrot & mango salad 205
crispy tofu with chili-soy sauce 186
mushroom & tofu broth 20
rice noodles with mushrooms & tofu 138
spiced mushrooms 172
tom yam gung 12
tomatoes
green papaya salad 200
red chicken with cherry tomatoes 117
sweet potato cakes with soy-tomato sauce 174
tuna & tomato salad with ginger dressing 60
tuna
spiced tuna in sweet & sour sauce 79
tuna & tomato salad with ginger dressing 60
turkey
egg noodle salad with lime & basil dressing 157

**V**
vegetables 165–191
vegetarian recipes
Asian vegetables with yellow bean sauce 184
carrot & mango salad 205
chilled avocado, lime & cilantro soup 22
coconut rice with pineapple 158
crisp pickled vegetables 166
eggplant & mushroom stuffed omelet 195
green papaya salad 200
hot & sour noodle salad 142
hot & sour noodles 145
jasmine rice with lemon & basil 156
mixed vegetables in peanut sauce 169
pineapple & cucumber salad 202
potatoes in creamed coconut 178
spiced cashew nut curry 168
spinach & ginger soup 26
sweet & sour potato stir-fry 177
Thai-style noodle röstis 148
vegetable & coconut curry 182
vegetable fritters with sweet chili dip 188
vegetarian spring rolls 59

**W**
won ton
chili-spiced shrimp won ton soup 10
steamed won ton bundles 47

**Y**
yellow curry
potato & spinach yellow curry 179